How To Study Difficult Passages Of The Bible!

Stephen W. Rogers

ISBN 0-9667521-5-5

Library of Congress 2003094805

A Product Of
Sain Publications
P. O. Box 616 • Pulaski, TN 38478
931-363-6905

Dedication

This book is dedicated to the members of the Washington Avenue Church of Christ in Evansville, IN who have longed to continually grow in knowledge of God's Word. These lessons were prepared to help our members become better students of the Bible. We have encouraged these brethren to learn to think for themselves and to use study aids to help them in their understanding of the Bible.

This material was first taught in our Bible Classes. The class size was limited to twenty students in an effort to urge the participants to feel free to openly participate in the study of and in the discussion of the texts. I have never taught Bible Classes where students have worked harder or grown more.

Every class has provided an opportunity to clarify and to improve these lessons. They have helped Mark Shifflet, one of our deacons, and me to expand the lessons and to clarify them. To all those students, "Thank you for your encouragements and challenges!"

I also dedicate this book to Mark Shifflet. We have had a great time studying God's Word together and have been wonderfully blessed to co-teach. Thanks Mark for your insights and your teaching abilities.

My prayer is that this book will assist teachers to have very provocative lessons to teach and will assist all students who diligently study this material to learn to think more for themselves and to rely less upon commentaries and upon other men's opinions. I want to see Christians become excellent interpreters of the Scripture.

May this book go forth to strengthen and to mature God's people!

Introduction

How To Study Difficult Passages Of The Bible is a very in-depth study. The first lesson sets forth principles for Bible study. In the following twelve lessons, the student is challenged to use those principles to grow in understanding how to study the Bible.

As Christians, we are urged to give diligent devotion to study of God's Word. II Timothy 2:15 in the NKJV says, "Be diligent to present yourself approved to God, a worker who does not need to be ashamed, rightly dividing the word of truth." Be motivated; put your heart into learning and loving God's wonderful Word!

As a teacher, I set some ground rules for the class. The class size was limited to twenty students in an effort to urge the participants to feel free to openly participate in the study of and in the discussion of the texts. Students were urged to study extensively outside the classroom. In lesson one, tools are identified that will assist them in the study. I encourage every teacher to help students purchase some of these tools. One strong encouragement is to discourage students from using commentaries during this study. I want them to learn to think for themselves without being led by commentator's thoughts.

A student workbook has been designed to assist in study of this material in a class setting. It is a barebones outline based upon the suggestions given in the first lesson.

Challenge yourself! Become a better student! Develop confidence that you CAN understand God's precious Word. Be eager and get started immediately!

Table Of Contents

Simple Suggestions For Successful Bible Study!

I. Introduction:

A. Studying The Bible Is Such A Thrilling Experience!
1. The more you delve into God's precious Word, the more exciting it becomes!

2. The more you study, the more you learn and are intrigued!

3. God intended for man to understand the Scriptures. Eph. 3:3-5

B. However, There ARE Passages Of The Bible And Biblical Truths That Are Difficult.
1. I Peter 1:10-12. Some may not see the whole picture.

2. II Peter 3:14-16. Some texts are harder than others.

3. Mark 9:32; Luke 18:34; Acts 1:6. Some Biblical Truths may be repulsive to our thinking.

C. Reactions That Different Students Have To Difficult Passages:

1. "I don't know where to start!"

2. "The Bible is just too hard to comprehend!"

3. "Someone else will have to help me."

4. "I'm just not smart enough to understand the Bible."

5. "It must be just for the 'clergy' to understand!"

D. Reasons Why Students Might Not Understand Passages.
   1. Lack of dedicated study!
      a. Many want "Microwave Interpretation!"
      b. You MUST invest time, energy, and mental faculties to learn!

   2. Preconceived ideas.
      a. One already has his mind made up about a teaching or a passage before he ever studies it.
      b. Biblical Truth may contradict your beliefs.
      c. Never attempt to mold God's Word to you!
      d. Rather, mold YOUR THINKING to It!
      e. This demands intellectual honesty on the part of the student!

   3. Influence of "Everybody has his own interpretation!"
      a. This axiom promotes the idea that "one idea is as good as another."

      b. It causes people to interpret the Bible to fit their own beliefs instead of seeking God's message.

      c. It makes students become "brain dead."

  4. Some passages are quite obscure and their meanings are not easily grasped.

II. Suggestions For Successful Bible Study

A. Approach The Bible With Fearful Respect And Desire To Know The Truth!

  1. I Thessalonians 2:13 "For this cause also thank we God without ceasing, because, when ye received the word of God which ye heard of us, ye received *it* not *as* the word of men, but as it is in truth, the word of God, which effectually worketh also in you that believe."

  2. John 17:17 "Sanctify them through thy truth: thy word is truth."

  3. Jn. 8:32 "And ye shall know the truth, and the truth shall make you free."

B. EXPECT To Understand!

  1. Many say, "You aren't supposed to understand everything!"

      a. They then quote Deuteronomy 29:29 "The secret things belong unto the LORD our God: but those things which are revealed belong unto us and to our children for ever, that we may do all the words of this law."

b. The "secret things" are unrevealed things!

c. Why did God give us the Bible if we cannot understand it?

d. Again, remember Paul's inspired affirmation about God's revelation, "when ye read, ye may understand my knowledge in the mystery of Christ." Eph. 3:4

2. A lack of familiarity with the whole message of the Bible (knowledge of the "Big Picture") can be a great hindrance in our understanding of Scripture. Hosea 4:6

3. Understanding may require lots of effort!

4. We need to get beyond "reading" and begin to "STUDY!"

a. II Timothy 2:15 "Give diligence; determine to rightly divide!"

b. Acts 17:11 The Bereans "searched the scriptures daily, whether those things were so."

5. The Scriptures have been written so that we can "know!" John 7:17; 8:32; 20:30,31; I John 5:13

6. Be like Ezra! Ezra 7:10 "For Ezra had prepared his heart to seek the law of the LORD, and to do *it*, and to teach in Israel statutes and judgments."

7. Be determined to understand it! Be tenacious!

C. Use Effective Study Tools!
  1. Before looking at specific tools, let's use an important analogy — TOOLS in a TOOLBOX.
     a. Different tools have completely different functions.
     b. Some people think hammers solve every problem. That is certainly not true.
     c. Illustrations of the use of different tools:
        1. Screwdrivers are for tightening or unloosing screws or bolts.
        2. Wrenches are used to tighten the nuts on bolts.
        3. Socket sets help to tighten bolts or unloosen them in an expeditious manner or to tighten bolts in hard-to-reach places.
        4. Saws are used for cutting.
        5. Hammers are used for nailing or removing nails.
     d. Sometimes you need to combine different tools to finish a project.
        1. You may use a screwdriver and a wrench to tighten a bolt.
        2. To cut a groove in a piece of wood or to break a piece of metal, you may use both a hammer and a chisel.
     e. Analogy in studying the Bible.
        1. There are many different tools to assist us in studying the Bible.
        2. We need to understand their functions and which problems each tool will be effective in solving.
        3. There are many times when combining several tools will be of great assistance in solving problem texts.

f. So, students are encouraged to think about this analogy as they study the Bible. You have a TOOLBOX filled with TOOLS to assist you to attack and solve difficult passages of the Bible. Know the different tools and their functions and use them wisely in understanding God's Word.

g. What ARE some of those tools?

2. **Different translations of the Bible.** (Sometimes they may help; sometimes they may only heighten your confusion; sometimes they may hinder)

a. Why is a study of translations helpful?

1. It gives different senses of what the word meant in the original language. It is somewhat like looking up a word in a thesaurus.

2. A word used in one translation may not give the correct sense of the original word; another translation may give the correct sense.

a. "Conversation" in the KJV in I Tim. 4:12 and Heb. 13:5.

b. Other translations use the words "in manner of life" or "life."

3. A passage might be easier for a student to grasp in one translation than in another.

b. Confusion may be heightened if translations do not use familiar words to the student.

1. One example is in the list of sins called the works of the flesh in Gal. 5:19.

a. The KJV and the ASV use the word "lasciviousness."

b. The RSV uses the word "licentiousnes."

c. The NIV uses the word "debauchery."

d. I have seen students come away from studying different translations and still have no understanding of the meaning of this word.

e. The word "lasciviousness" means "anything that tends to, leads to, or that is involved in the promotion of lust." Thayer defines this word as "indecent bodily movements" or "unchaste handling of males and females." Thayer, Joseph Henry. *Thayer's Greek-English Lexicon of the New Testament*, Grand Rapids, MI: Zondervan, 1974, pp. 79,80.

2. Another example is found in Rom. 3:25; I Jn. 2:2, 4:10.

a. The KJV and the ASV use the word "propitiation."

b. The NIV uses the word "atonement" or "atoning sacrifice."

c. The RSV uses the word "expiation."

d. Many students still do not grasp the true concept of this word.

e. The idea of these words is that an acceptable sacrifice is made (here, the ONLY sacrifice that God would accept was the Death of Christ) whereby God's anger or wrath against sin could be appeased.

c. Be aware of the use of "*Italics*" in English translations of the Bible!

1. In most writing, italics is used for EMPHASIS!

2. In the Bible, it suggests that the word is NOT IN the original text!

3. The italicized word was inserted to help give the sense of the text.

d. Realize that translation is not always easy.

1. Think about how difficult idioms are for translators.

2. Examples:

a. "Give up."

1. What does it mean?

2. "I quit!" "I do not wish to continue."

3. Look up the words "give" and the word "up" in the dictionary and try to come up with the idea of "I quit."

b. "Pig in a poke."

1. What does it mean?

2. It means you were taken advantage of, you were cheated, or you were deceived.

4. Look up the words "pig" and "poke" in the dictionary and try to come up with the idea of "being deceived."

3. **Original Texts**: Hebrew and Greek.
   a. You DO NOT have to know those languages.
   b. There are many books that will assist you as you seek to understand the original meanings of the texts!
   c. **Grammars** — Machen; Mounce
   d. **Lexicons** — Thayer's; Arndt and Gingrich; Brown, Driver, and Briggs.
   e. **Expositor's Dictionaries** — Vine's; Kittle's.
   e. **Word Study Books** — A.T. Robertson; Vincent's, Wuest's.

4. **Concordances**. (Books or computer programs)
   a. They list every time a word is used in the Scriptures.
   c. They give the word and the original word and its meanings.

5. **Bible Dictionaries**.

6. **Commentaries**.
   a. Remember that they are written by men!
   b. Always ask, "What is the author's theology?"

7. **Bible Encyclopedias**.
   a. International Standard Bible Encyclopedia.
   b. McClintock and Strong.

8. **Church History Books**.

9. **Bible Geography Books.**

10. **Consider The Context!**
    a. WHO wrote it?
    b. TO WHOM was it written?
    c. What is the SETTING and the circumstances of its writing?
    d. What do the WORDS MEAN in that setting?
    e. What has ALREADY BEEN SPOKEN about this topic or event earlier?
       1. Sometimes we need to look at the words of the immediate passage before we go a broader context.
       2. Consider parallel texts. For example, many events in Jesus' life are recorded in two or more Gospel accounts.
    f. Broader contexts:
       1. The immediate thoughts in the specific verse.
       2. Paragraphs.
       3. Chapters.
       4. The specific Bible book and its messages.
       5. Other books written to the same recipients.
       6. The context of the different Dispensations (Patriarchal, Mosaic, and Christian).
       7. Testaments (New or Old).
       8. The whole Bible context. Sometimes an immediate focus upon the whole Bible context shows the fallaciousness of a possible interpretation.

11. **Uses of Language!**
    a. **Grammar**.
        1. It is AMAZING how many students have a strong dislike of "DREADED GRAMMAR!"
        2. And yet, this is such a VITAL tool to comprehension of anything we read, particularly the Bible!
        3. Specific grammar concerns:
            a. Parts of speech.
                1. Nouns
                2. Pronouns
                3. Verbs
                4. Adverbs
                5. Adjectives
                6. Conjunctions
            b. Learn to diagram [parse] sentences.
        4. Try to get a grasp of the basics of Greek words.
            a. The meaning of different **tenses** of Greek verbs:
                1. Present — an action presently occurring or continual action.
                2. Aorist — Point action, typically in the past; however, if used in the subjunctive mood it refers to a point action that may occur in the future.
                3. Future — what will happen in the future.
                4. Perfect — action completed in the past with continuing results.

5. Imperfect tense — continued action during past time.
6. Pluperfect — action completed in the past up to a prescribed limit of time.

b. **Cases**
   1. Nominative — subject of a sentence.
   2. Genitive — prepositional phrase denoting possession.
   3. Dative — prepositional phrase used as an indirect object.
   4. Accusative — direct object of a verb.
   5. Vocative — direct address.

c. **Person**
   1. First person singular — "I"
   2. Second person singular — "you"
   3. Third person singular — "he", "she" or "it"
   4. First person plural — "we"
   5. Second person plural — "you"
   6. Third person plural — "they"

d. **Voice**
   1. Active — the subject of the sentence performs the action.
   2. Middle — the subject performs the action upon himself.

           3.   Passive — another person does the action to you.

    e. **Mood**

           1.   Indicative — statement of fact; assertion of fact in contrast with a command or a wish.

           2.   Imperative — command.

           3.   Subjunctive — the action of the verb may possibly happen; it is possible but not certain.

b. **Literal or figurative use of words**.

    1. "Door"

        a. Literal door:

           1.   John 18:16,17

           2.   Acts 5:9

           3.   Acts 12:6

           4.   Acts 12:13,16

        b. Figurative:

           1.   Christ, the door to Heaven. (Fellowship with Christ). John 10:1,2,7,9

           2.   Opportunity.

               a. I Corinthians 16:9

               b. II Corinthians 2:12

               c. Colossians 4:3

           3.   Privilege to have faith! Acts 14:27

    2. Advice when considering the literal or figurative use of a word:

        a. Always begin by attempting a literal interpretation.

           1.   Generally it will be evident if a word or phrase is used

figuratively instead of literally.

2. Examples:
   a. If a literal interpretation involves an impos--sibility.
   b. If a literal interpretation makes the Bible contradict itself.
   c. If a literal interpretation demands actions that are wrong.

b. If you interchange a figurative interpretation for a literal passage or a literal interpretation for a figurative passage, you will distort and miss the meaning of the message.

c. **Figures of speech**!
   1. **Simile**. (Something is "like" or "as" another thing). Matthew 23:27
   2. **Parable**. (An earthly story with a heavenly meaning). "The Sower Sowing Seed." Matthew 13:1-9; 18-23
   3. **Metaphor**. (Something is another thing. "Like" or "as" are not used!)
      a. Matthew 26:26-28 "This is my body." "This is my blood"
      b. Jn. 15:5 "I am the vine, ye are the branches:"
   4. **Allegory**. (Symbolic representation). Galatians 4:21-5:1
   5. **Metonymy**. (Substitution of one word for another).
      a. "Moses" is substituted for the "Law of Moses." Ac. 15:21

      b.   Christians are said to have received the "Holy Spirit" when they received the supernatural gifts that He provided through the Apostle's hands. Ac. 19:6

   6. **Synecdoche**. (Substituting parts for the whole)

      a.   "Faith" or "Belief" used to refer to obedience to all Christ commands. Eph. 2:8; Jn. 3:16; Ac. 16:31

      b.   "Break bread" used to refer to the "Lord's Supper." Ac. 20:7

   7. **Type and antitype**.

      a.   Use of a physical event in the O.T. that points to a spiritual truth or event in the N.T.

      b.   Example: Noah and his family were saved by the literal waters of the Flood; sinners are saved by the "waters" of baptism. I Pet. 3:20,21

D. General Guidelines For Successful Biblical Interpretation.

   1. Attempt to let the Bible be its own commentary!

   2. Use COMMON Sense!

      a.   This involves thinking!

      b.   Take your interpretation to its logical conclusion.

         1. Does I Tim. 2:4 affirm universalism?

        2.   "Who will have all men to be saved, and to come unto the knowledge of the truth."

        3.   Does this imply that all WILL BE SAVED or that He desires for all to come to Him for salvation?

   c.   Does my interpretation sound like the God of the Bible?

   d.   I Thessalonians 5:21 "Prove all things; hold fast that which is good."

3.   Avoid letting a word in a passage cause you to so focus on that one word and its use in other passages that you miss the context and meaning of the passage that you are studying!

   a.   "Ark" may refer to the "Ark of the Covenant" in the Tabernacle or later in the Temple; it may also refer to Noah's Ark.

   b.   "Temple" may refer to the place of Jewish worship where God's presence resided in Israel; it may refer to Solomon's Temple, Zerubbabel's Temple, or to Herod's Temple. It may also refer to the "temple" of our body, I Cor. 6:19, or to the church. I Cor. 3:16

4.   If your interpretation of a difficult passage contradicts other passages, keep these truths in mind.

   a.   God does not contradict Himself.

   b.   If you believe there is a contradiction, the confusion is in your understanding, not in God's Revelation.

        1.   He cannot lie! Titus 1:2; Hebrews 6:18

2. He is not the author of confusion!

3. Contradictions are in MY understanding; NOT IN GOD'S WORD!

c. Be committed to further study.

5. Does a passage make an explicit statement of truth or does it contain implications of truth beyond the immediate statement?

a. **Explicit statements**.

1. John 8:24 "I said therefore unto you, that ye shall die in your sins: for if ye believe not that I am he, ye shall die in your sins."

2. Hebrews 11:6 "But without faith it is impossible to please him: for he that cometh to God must believe that he is, and that he is a rewarder of them that diligently seek him."

b. **Implicit statements**:

1. Hebrews 7:12-14 The Law of Moses asserted that the Priests were to be of the tribe of Levi. The very fact that Jesus is NOW our High Priest proves that we are NOT under the Law of Moses; rather we are now under the Law of Christ, the New Testament.

2. John 13:3-17 Jesus washing His disciples' feet was not just an act of washing feet. He was teaching them about servitude, about being willing to humble oneself and to serve others.

3. Mark 16:15,16 The statement "he that believeth not shall be damned"

implies that one without faith will be damned, and that one who refuses to be baptized is in reality an unbeliever who will be damned also.

4. II Thessalonians 1:6-9 Those who have not heard, and those who have heard but who refuse to obey the Gospel will be lost!

6. What are the implications of this passage for me?
    a. What can I learn about God's Will for MY life?
    b. What responsibilities can I grasp for my life?
    c. How will understanding this passage help me in studying other difficult passages?

III. Suggestions As We Study Difficult Passages Of The Bible.
A. Never Use Difficult Passages As The Basis For New Or Novel Doctrines.

B. "Think Outside Your Box!"
    1. This has been a "catch phrase" during the 1990's and early 2000's.

    2. Laugh Parade cartoon: A woman stands talking to her cat and pointing to its litter box. She says, "I admire your independent spirit, but no thinking outside the box."

3.   Some students are lazy and are not willing to think beyond what they have previously thought or heard.

4.   Other students are too rigid; they are not willing to consider that their views might be wrong; they are fearful that their conclusions might be challenged and are unwilling to change any views they hold.

5.   The suggestion to "think outside your box" is not urging people to try to deny God's Truths or to seek to do things contradictory to the Bible. It is an encouragement that we do not just become "brain dead;" rather students should seek to think in-depth because of a fervent desire to truly understand God's Word!

C.   Never Be Rigidly Dogmatic About Your Conclusions If Another's Interpretation Does Not Contradict Biblical Doctrines.
   1.   If we have different conclusions, it does not imply that the other person is liberal, dishonest, or disrespectful of the Bible.

   2.   We are not talking about one hating the Truth and rejecting It!
      a.   We are not talking about "agreeing to disagree" about doctrine.
      b.   We are suggesting that brethren may have different views about non-essential matters.

    c. Examples:
       1. What kind of fruit did Adam and Eve eat from the Tree? Gen. 3:3-6
       2. Where did Adam and Eve get the skins for their clothes? Did they just kill animals? Or was it the result of sacrificing animals?

   3. If we do not have a clear answer, do not get frustrated or waste a lot of time upon the thought!
      a. Example: what kind of fruit did Adam and Eve eat?
      b. Do not focus upon unanswerable questions to the neglect of the MESSAGE!

D. Avoid Being So Obsessed With Problem Passages That You Miss The Clear Truths Of God's Word And Neglect Personal Applications Of Those Truths!

IV. Responsibilities For This Class.

A. The Teacher Will Be The Class Facilitator.

B. Students Are To Study During The Week And To Come Prepared To Seek Answers For The Problem Texts.
   1. Determine what the issues are. "Why is this a problem text?"

   2. What are possible interpretations? Take those interpretations to their logical conclusion.

3. Evaluate which "tools" you will use to solve this problem.

4. Study Biblical usage of words, the immediate context, and consider the passage in light of the whole Biblical context.

5. Decide upon what you believe to be the most plausible interpretation. Be prepared to explain that interpretation.

6. Students are encouraged to be studious, to desire to learn how to study, and to be respectful and courteous to other students during this study!

C. Note: I Have Used The King James Version Except When Another Translation Has Been Identified.

Suggested Study Material:
"Tools, Hermeneutical Principles, Methods And Approaches Needed In Studying Difficult Texts," by Goebel Music. From *Difficult Texts Of The New Testament Explained*, edited by Wendell Winkler. 1981 Forth Worth Lectures, pp. 6-16.

How To Study The Bible by Roy Deaver. 1976.

When Is An Example Binding? by Thomas B. Warren. 1975.

ASSIGNMENT:

A. Why Is The Word "Lord" In All Caps In Gen. 2:4, 5,7,8,9,15,16,18,19,21,22, et. al."
    1. The purpose of this assignment is to encourage the students to begin to learn how to use a concordance.

    2. Although a quite simple assignment, it gives them a feeling of accomplishment that they can dig and learn very quickly.

B. Grammar Problems:
    1. Use of the word "So" or "Thus" in Romans 11:25-27 and Romans 5:12.

    2. Use of "Unworthy" or "Unworthily" in Acts 13:46 and I Corinthians 11:27,29.

Grammar Problems – "So" Or "Thus," "Worthy" And "Unworthily"

Introduction:

A. Discussing Your Assignment: Why Is The Word "Lord" In All Caps In Gen. 2:4,5,7,8,9,15,16,18, 19,21,22, et. al."

1. This is the Hebrew word "YHWH" which is translated "Jehovah" in some translations and "LORD" in other translations.

2. To Whom Does "LORD" refer?

   a. Most people would immediately say, "It refers to God, the Father."

   b. Study Deut. 6:4 "Hear, O Israel: The LORD our God *is* one LORD:"

      1. "LORD" is the word "YHWH."

      2. Also, look up the word "God."

         a. It is the plural Hebrew word "Elohim."

         b. This is the same word used in Gen. 1:1.

         c. We can readily see that it is plural in the English texts: Gen. 1:26; 3:22; 11:7; Is. 6:8.

   3. So, to WHOM does "LORD" refer?

   4. It refers to all three members of the Godhead, the Father, the Son, and the Holy Spirit.

5. Interestingly, this is the passage that Moslems and others who deny the deity of Jesus Christ and the Holy Spirit use to defend their false teaching.
   a. They say, "There is only ONE God!"
   b. They claim that Christianity is polytheism.
   c. Such could not be more wrong!
   d. Polytheism believes in many different kinds of gods, all struggling against each other for control and dominance.
   e. Christianity is based upon three distinct Divine Beings, all having the same nature and will. They work together in total harmony.

B. Learning Grammar In Early Life Is SO Important To Comprehension, Whether In Listening, Reading Secular Material, Or In Reading, Interpreting, and Understanding The Word Of God!

C. Examples Of Grammar And Communication.
   1. "Lookout Ahead"
      a. Gary Larson's "Farside" Cartoon, March 20, 1990.
         1. A road winds around a huge mountain.
         2. A sign near the top of the mountain as one goes up a crooked, narrow,

mountain road reads, "Lookout ahead."

   3. What would you immediately assume?
- b. Assumptions:
  1. There would be a scenic view alongside the road?
  2. This is a warning of danger you are approaching?
- c. In the cartoon, one rounds the crest of the mountain and there is another sign, "LOOKOUT!" The road ends and a car is flying off the mountain to land on a pile of cars that have previously flown off the mountain and now lie in a heap at the bottom of the mountain.

2. "Bear"
- a. Noun
  1. Animal
  2. Chicago Bears
  3. Central High School Bears in Evansville, IN.
  4. Gummy Bears
  5. "Bear" of a person (metaphoric use of the word)
- b. Verb
  1. Carry a load.
  2. Have a baby.

3. Born Loser: "Cold Turkey"; November 26, 2000.
- a. The following is a discussion between the "Born Loser", Brutus Thornapple and his neighbor.

b. "It's not going to be easy, but this time I really mean it — I'm quitting cold turkey!"

c. "Well, good for you! I must admit, I didn't even know you were a smoker."

d. "What do you mean? I don't smoke!"

e. "Then what were you talking about giving up cold turkey?"

f. "Like I said, I'm giving up cold turkey..."

g. "I'm sick of eating leftovers from Thanksgiving dinner!"

4. You write on a resume, "You would be **lucky** to have this person to work for you."

   a. It might suggest that you would be "lucky" to have them.

   b. It might also suggest that you would be "lucky if they would really be a "worker" at all!

5. After returning home from worship, my cousin Sharon asked my Aunt Reniva on Sunday afternoon "Mom, who is the 'dumb brother' we sang about at church this morning?' My aunt had no clue what she meant. Finally she understood. Sharon was talking about the song, "Are you sowing the seed of the kingdom, brother?"

6. A little boy had been fascinated by the sermon he heard on angels. As he was telling a friend about it, they got into an argument. The little friend insisted that all angels have wings, but the little boy disagreed. "It isn't true,' he

insisted, "Our preacher says that some of them are strangers in <u>underwares</u>." (Heb. 13:2)

7. Newspaper headlines.
    a. "Expert Says Police Begin Campaign To Run Down Jaywalkers"
    b. "Miners Refuse To Work After Death"
    c. "Two Sisters Reunited After 18 Years At Checkout Counter"
    d. "Red Tape Holds Up New Bridges"
    e. "Local High School Dropouts Cut In Half"
    f. "Typhoon Rips Through Cemetery; Hundreds Killed"

8. Rom. 6:17 "But God be thanked, that ye **were** the servants of sin, **but** ye **have obeyed** from the heart that form of doctrine which was delivered you."
    a. The Romans USED TO BE slaves to sin.
    b. However, they have obeyed from their heart (with total sincerity) God's teachings.
    c. Now, they are slaves of Christ! 18,19,22

9. Galatians 3:26,27 "For ye **are** all the children of God by faith in Christ Jesus. [27]For as many of you as **have been baptized** into Christ have put on Christ."
    a. The Galatians **are now** the children of God because of their continuing faith in Christ.
    b. Why are they **now** God's children? Because they **have been baptized** into Christ in the past!

c. Faith does not tell how they became Christians; it describes the life they now life since they have been baptized into Christ!

I. **The Problem: "What does "SO" or "THUS" mean?**
A. **The Texts**:
1. **Rom. 11:25-27** "For I would not, brethren, that ye should be ignorant of this mystery, lest ye should be wise in your own conceits; that blindness in part is happened to Israel, until the fulness of the Gentiles be come in. ²⁶And *SO* all Israel shall be saved: as it is written, There shall come out of Sion the Deliverer, and shall turn away ungodliness from Jacob: ²⁷For this *is* my covenant unto them, when I shall take away their sins." KJV

2. **Rom. 5:12** "Wherefore, as by one man sin entered into the world, and death by sin; and *SO* death passed upon all men, for that all have sinned:" KJV

B. **Possible Solutions** To The Problem:
1. **Romans 11:25-27**
a. "I don't know WHAT it means!"
b. There comes a time in the future when every Jew is going to be saved.
1. This would be the interpretation if "so" is a conjunction.
2. This is the premillennial view. (By the way, that does not necessarily make it wrong! The question is, "IS

it a wrong interpretation or conclusion?")

3. Those who hold this view believe that the State of Israel is so important to the world.
4. This view is held by a majority of politicians and premillennial teachers.
5. During the 1970's, Mark Shifflet's grandmother sent money to support Israel's survival.

c. Israel will be saved by faith in the New Covenant, just as Gentiles have been and will be saved.
   1. This would be the interpretation if "so" is an adverb.
   2. Adverbially, it would mean, "in the same way."

2. **Romans 5:12**
   a. "I don't know WHAT it means!"
   b. Because Adam sinned, he died physically; thus, all men die physically.
      1. It is true that physical death came to Adam and Eve because of their sin in the Garden of Eden. Gen. 2:17
      2. All die physically because of Adam's sin. I Cor. 15:21,22 "For since by man *came* death, by man *came* also the resurrection of the dead. [22]For as in Adam all die, even so in Christ shall all be made alive."
   c. Because Adam sinned, everybody is born a sinner.

        1.   This would be the interpretation if "so" is a conjunction.

        2.   It could be translated "therefore."

    d.   Every person who becomes a sinner becomes one exactly as Adam did — when he sins in his own life!

        1.   This would be the interpretation if "so" is an adverb.

        2.   Adverbially, it would mean, "in the same way."

C. Tools To Use In Solving This Problem.

1.   Different **translations**.

2.   Study the **grammar** of the words "so" or "thus."

3.   The use of "so" or "thus" in **other passages**.

4.   The **immediate context** of Romans 11:25-27 And Romans 5:12.

5.   The whole **Bible context**.

D. Using Our Tools To Solve The Problem.

1.   Different **translations**.

    a.   Rom. 11:26

        1.   The KJV, NKJV, ASV, NIV and RSV all use the word "so."

        2.   The English Version for the Deaf says "that is how."

    b.   Rom. 5:12

        1.   The KJV, ASV, RSV and English Version for the Deaf use "so."

    2.   The NIV says "in this way."

    3.   The NKJV says "thus."

2. **Grammar**: What kind of word is **"SO"** or **"Thus"**?

  a. **Pronoun?**

    1. How could it be used as a pronoun?

    2. **"You need to get the yard raked! Do so as soon as possible."**

    3. "I'll get done in a week or so!"

    4. "It costs $100 or so!"

  b. **Conjunction?**

    1. If used as a conjunction, what would it mean?

    2. **"Therefore,"** "Consequently"

    3. **He was speeding, so he got a ticket.**

  c. **Adjective?**

    1. If used in the adjective form, what would it mean?

    2. **"True." "What he said was not so!"**

    3. "Just as they should be." "His writing was just so!"

  d. **Adverb?**

    1. If used as an adverb, what would it mean?

    2. **"In the SAME WAY;"** "Thus;" or **"To a GREAT DEGREE."**

    3. **"I am SO happy!"**

    4. **"I worked hard and so did she!"**

  e. Can I KNOW if it is a conjunction, adjective, or an adverb?

    1. How is it used in the sentence?

    2. In Greek, it is often a different word!

    3. You DO NOT HAVE TO KNOW GREEK to find out the meaning of the original word!

      a.   Young's Analytical Concordance.

      b.   Strong's Analytical Concordance.

      c.   Quick Verse Bible Program.

      d.   Online Bible Program.

3. **Other passages** where "SO" is used:

   a. "So" sometimes translated a completely different Greek word.

     1. "Τοῦτο" (touto) meaning "this."

     2. Jn. 11:28 "And when she had **so** said, she went her way, and called Mary her sister secretly, saying, The Master is come, and calleth for thee."

     3. Jn. 20:20 "And when he had **so** said, he showed unto them *his* hands and his side."

     4. Rom. 12:20 "Therefore if thine enemy hunger, feed him; if he thirst, give him drink: for in **so** doing thou shalt heap coals of fire on his head." (ASV has "so"; NIV has "this")

   b. Translations of the same Greek word used in Rom. 11:26 and 5:12 — "οὕτως" (houtoos).

     1 Mt. 5:12 "Rejoice, and be exceeding glad: for great *is* your reward in heaven: for **so** persecuted they the prophets which were before you."

     2. Mt. 5:16 "Let your light **so** shine before men, that they may see your good works, and glorify your Father which is in heaven."

3. Mt. 6:30 "Wherefore, if God **so** clothes the grass of the field, which to day is, and to morrow is cast into the oven, *shall he* not much more *clothe* you, O ye of little faith?"
4. Mt. 7:12 "Therefore all things whatsoever ye would that men should do to you, do ye even **so** to them: for this is the law and the prophets."
5. Mt. 12:40 "For as Jonas was three days and three nights in the whale's belly; **so** shall the Son of man be three days and three nights in the heart of the earth."
6. Ac. 1:11 "Which also said, Ye men of Galilee, why stand ye gazing up into heaven? this same Jesus, which is taken up from you into heaven, shall **so** come in like manner as ye have seen him go into heaven."
7. I Cor. 11:28 "But let a man examine himself, and **so** let him eat of *that* bread, and drink of *that* cup."

4. **Immediate context** of the passages.
   a. Romans 11:25-27
      1. Romans 1-8 All men are justified by faith in Christ.
      2. Romans 9-11 The relationship of God to the nation of Israel and to the Gentiles.
      3. Outline of chapters 9-11:
         a. 9:1-5 Paul's love for the Jews.

      b.   9:6-29 God's justice in rejecting Israel.
- 1. His sovereign right to choose Isaac and Jacob. 6-18
- 2. The Jews chastised for questioning God's sovereign right to choose. 19-29

      c.   9:30-33 God's right to reject Jews and to choose Gentiles.

      d.   10:1-3 Paul wishes the Jews would understand God's means of justification.

      e.   Justification through Christ brought an end to the Law. 10:4-10

      f.   Justification is available to all who believe in Christ! 10:11-17

      g.   Many remain in unbelief. 10:18-21

      h.   11:1-6 A remnant of believing Jews remain.

      i.   11:7-10 Israel as a nation has been rejected.

      j.   11:11-16 Israelites can STILL be saved.

      k.   11:17-24 Gentiles are described as an engrafted branch.

      l.   11:25-32 Salvation is available to ALL on the SAME terms!

      m.   11:33-36 The riches of God's wisdom!

  b.   Romans 5:12
- 1. All have sinned! Rom. 1-3
  - a. Gentiles have sinned. 1
  - b. Jews have too! 2,3

2. Justification with God is available by faith!
   a. 4:1-8 Abraham was justified by faith.
   b. 4:9-25 All sinners, Jews or Gentiles, are justified by faith.
   c. 5:1-11 Peace and hope are available only in Christ.
   d. 5:22-21 Jesus' death more than overcomes the effects of sin!

5. The **whole Biblical context**.
   a. There HAS NEVER BEEN and NEVER WILL BE a time when all people of a nation will be "saved people"!
   b. Mt. 7:13,14 "Enter ye in at the strait gate: for wide *is* the gate, and broad *is* the way, that leadeth to destruction, and many there be which go in thereat: [14]Because strait *is* the gate, and narrow *is* the way, which leadeth unto life, and few there be that find it."
   c. Judgment is an individual event!
      1. Ecc. 12:13,14 "Let us hear the conclusion of the whole matter: Fear God, and keep his commandments: for this *is* the whole *duty* of man. [14]For God shall bring every work into judgment, with every secret thing, whether *it be* good, or whether *it be* evil."
      2. II Cor. 5:10 "For we must all appear before the judgment seat of Christ; that every one may receive the things *done* in *his* body, according to that

he hath done, whether *it be* good or bad."

3. Rom. 14:10 "we shall all stand before the judgment seat of Christ."

4. Gal. 6:7 "Be not deceived; God is not mocked: for whatsoever a man soweth, that shall he also reap."

5. Rev. 22:12 "And, behold, I come quickly; and my reward *is* with me, to give every man according as his work shall be."

E. The Correct Interpretation Of "SO" Is Readily Seen By 3 Critical Criteria. It Is NOT A Conjunction Meaning "Therefore;" It Is An Adverb That Means "In The Same Way."

1. The adverbial use of "So!"

2. The context of Romans.

3. The Biblical emphasis on the individual nature of judgment.

II. "Unworthy And Unworthily."
A. The Problem:
1. What does "unworthily" mean?

2. Many Christians believe they must be in a certain state, have a certain state of holiness, or must have avoided sin during the week before they are qualified to partake of the Lord's Supper on Sunday.

3.   Is ANYONE truly "worthy" to partake of this Divine memorial?
   a.   What if you gave in to a temptation and sinned during the week?
   b.   What if you are really struggling with temptation?
   c.   What if you sinned during the week? That morning?
      1.   What if you yelled at your children this morning?
      2.   What if you sped on the way to worship?

B.   **Possible Interpretations:**
1.   "What's the problem?"

2.   "I don't know WHAT it means."

3.   "Christians must be almost sinless before they are WORTHY to partake of the Lord's Supper."

4.   "This word refers to the ATTITUDE of those who are remembering Christ and HOW they take the Lord's Supper."

C.   **Tools To Use In Solving This Problem.**
1.   **Grammar**.

2.   **Study of words**.

3.   Study **different translations**.

D. **Using Our Tools To Solve The Problem.**
1. **Grammar**: use of adjectives and adverbs.
   a. "Bad"
      1. He is a BAD guy! (adjective)
      2. He acted BADLY! (adverb)
   b. "Good"
      1. He is a GOOD man! (adjective)
      2. He acted GOOD. (adverb). (This is not considered to be correct English by many grammaticians).
      3. "Charlie The Tuna" commercial. "They don't want tunas with GOOD taste (adjective); they want tunas that taste GOOD (adverb)!"

2. **Study of the words** in the texts:
   a. **"Unworthy"**
      1. It is only used twice in the KJV.
      2. Ac. 13:46 "Then Paul and Barnabas waxed bold, and said, It was necessary that the word of God should first have been spoken to you: but seeing ye put it from you, and judge yourselves **unworthy** of everlasting life, lo, we turn to the Gentiles."
         a. "Unworthy" comes from two Greek words, "οὐκ ἀξίους" (ouk axious) meaning "not worthy."
         b. This is used in the sense of an adjective.
         c. Adjectives modify nouns. They denote the quality of the thing named!

3. The other time is I Cor. 6:2. "Do ye not know that the saints shall judge the world? and if the world shall be judged by you, are ye **unworthy** to judge the smallest matters?"

   a. This is the word "ἀνάξιοι" (anaxioi).

   b. This is a noun used in an adjective sense.

   c. Are you so "unworthy," so "incompetent", so "inadequate" that you cannot make decisions about the smallest disagreements among yourselves?

b. **"Unworthily"**

   1. I Cor. 11:27 "Wherefore whosoever shall eat this bread, and drink *this* cup of the Lord, **unworthily**, shall be guilty of the body and blood of the Lord."

      a. This is the Greek word "ἀναξίως" (anaxioos).

      b. It is an adverb.

      c. It talks about a wrong way that the Lord's Supper can be taken or observed.

      d. When Christians treat it as a common meal and do not think about Christ's Body and Blood, they do so "unworthily."

   2. I Cor. 11:29 "For he that eateth and drinketh unworthily, eateth and drinketh damnation to himself, not discerning the Lord's body."

       a. This is the same Greek word as in 11:27.

       b. It is not found in many Greek MSS.

3. Adverbs serve as the modifiers of verbs, adjectives, others adverbs, prepositions or phrases. They suggest the quality of something or how an action has been done.

4. How could one partake of the Lord's Supper "unworthily?"

       a. The Corinthians were not observing this holy Memorial together, showing their fellowship in Christ. I Cor. 11:21,33

       b. It had become as a common meal for the hungry to eat. Some were full; others had nothing to eat. I Cor. 11:21,34

       c. Some think they were using intoxicants. I Cor. 11:21

       d. They had totally ignored the purpose of the Memorial — remembrance of Christ! I Cor. 11:24,25,29

       e. The results of their misuse of the Supper: Some were spiritually sick, others had died! I Cor. 11:30

3. **Translations**:

    a. Ac. 13:46

       1. The KJV, ASV, NKJV, RSV use "unworthy.

2. The NIV says "do not consider yourselves worthy"
3. The English Version for the Deaf says "not worthy."
  b. I Cor. 11:27
1. The KJV uses "unworthily."
2. The ASV, NIV, NKJV use "in an unworthy manner."
3. The RSV uses "in an unworthy manner."
4. The English Version for the Deaf says "in a way that is not worthy of it."
  c. I Cor. 11:29
1. The KJV and NKJV use "unworthily."
2. The ASV, RSV, and NIV omit this word, simply emphasizing that one does not discern or recognize the Lord's body.
3. The English Version for the Deaf says "without recognizing the body."

E. The Word "Unworthily" Or The Phrase "In An Unworthy Manner" Do Not Demand Perfection Of The Observer Of The Lord's Supper; They Emphasize The Attitude Christians Should Have As They Observe The Lord's Supper;

Conclusion:
A. The Main Point Of This Study: We Must Understand The Kinds Of Words We Are Interpreting And Ask, "What Do Those Kinds Of Words Mean?"

B.   This Is CRITICAL To Correct Interpretation!

C.   Amazingly, Many False Doctrines And Misconceptions Are Rooted In Such Cases Of Incorrect Interpretation Of Words!

Suggested Study Material:
"Difficult Texts From Romans And Galatians. Romans 11:25-29: What Is 'The Fulness Of The Gentiles' and What Does 'So All Israel Shall Be Saved' Mean?," by Roy H. Lanier, Sr. From *Difficult Texts Of The New Testament Explained*, edited by Wendell Winkler. 1981 Forth Worth Lectures, pp. 197-201.

ASSIGNMENT: Parable Of The Unjust Steward. Lk. 16:1-13
A.   What IS A "Parable?"

B.   What Is The PURPOSE Of Parables?

C.   Why Is The Man Called "The Unjust Steward?"

D.   What Is The Real Lesson Of This Parable?

Parables:
The Unjust Steward

Introduction:

A. In This Lesson, One Parable Will Be Used As An Example Of Trying To Find The Real Meaning Of Parables And Of Understanding The Attendant Problems That Can Occur.

B. We Will Study "The Parable Of The Unjust Steward."

I. **The Scriptures: Lk. 16:1-13**

II. **The Problem: This Parable Is SO Troublesome To Many!**

A. Is Jesus Commending Devious Behavior?

B. What Was The Steward Doing And What Is His Motivation?

C. What Are Christians To Gain From This Parable?

III. Tools To Use In Solving This Problem:
   A. **Understanding "Parables!"**

   B. The **Immediate Context**.

   C. **Meaning Of Words**.

   D. Detailed **Study Of The Parable**.

   E. **Message Of The Parable**.

IV. Solutions To The Problem. Using Tools To Solve The Problem.
   A. **Understanding "Parables!"**
      1. **What IS a parable?**
         a. Many have defined a parable as "an earthly narrative with a heavenly meaning."
         b. The term parable comes from the Greek word "παραβολή" (parabola) that means "place by the side of" or "to throw beside."
         c. It is a "comparison." Parables compare earthly people or events with spiritual applications!

      2. **What is the purpose of parables?**
         a. They aroused curiosity.

    b.   They caused people to stay interested until Jesus drove home the point of His message.

    c.   He put GREAT truths in "easy-to-remember" capsules.

    d.   Mt. 13:10-17.[1]

        1.   They VEIL Truth from enemies and scoffers.

        2.   They UNVEIL Truth for sincere seekers of Truth!

        3.   They ELICIT a condemnation from His enemies of their lifestyle.

        4.   They SOLICIT devotion to God from those desiring the Truth.

        5.   They EMPHASIZE deeper understanding of eternal Truths.

        6.   They IMMORTALIZE Truths in the hearts of the world forever!

3. **How to interpret parables.**

    a.   Keep in mind that they ARE Parables!

        1.   They are not fables!

            a.   Fables are just made-up stories.

                1.   Things in them can be very unrealistic; for example, they may tell of animals or trees talking.

                2.   Aesop's Fables are an example:

                    a.   "The Hare and the Tortoise"

                    b.   "The Lion and the Hare"

                    c.   "The Hares and the Frogs"

3.   "Humpty Dumpty"
b.   Parables deal with realistic happenings (there are no talking animals or trees).
2.   They are not proverbs!
a.   Proverbs merely state widely accepted axioms; they are not 100% set in concrete rules.
b.   A parable must include a likeness or similitude of some vividly recognized experience of life.
3.   They are not allegories.
a.   Parables and allegories are both comparisons.
b.   However, an allegory uses direct personification of ideas or attributes. It transfers or applies the properties of one thing **to** another.   Its interpretation is usually self-evident.
c.   A parable compares one thing **with** another. It may need explanation (which is what Jesus does in many instances).
d.   Examples of allegories:
1.   C.S. Lewis' *Chronicles of Narnia* (Lion, Witch & Wardrobe — It's fairly obvious that the Lion is an allegory of Christ).
2.   Gal. 4:21-31 Hagar and Ishmael represented the bondage under the Law of

Moses; Sarah and Isaac represented freedom under the Law of Christ.

    e.   The difference between a parable and an allegory is important because in interpreting a parable, the point is not to try and figure out who all the characters represent. In interpreting an allegory, each item in the story represents someone else.

4.   Example of an attempt to allegorize a parable:[2]

    a.   The rich man — God

    b.   The unrighteous steward — the scribes and Pharisees

    c.   The accusations — the protestations of the prophets and last of all, of Christ.

    d.   The day of accounting — the first advent of Christ.

    e.   The lowering of the bills — the corruption of God's law by the religious leaders.

    f.   The impending eviction of the steward — the impending removal of Israel as a chosen nation.

    g.   The corruption of the debtors — the ruin of the vast majority of Israel by their leaders.

    h.   The lord's commendation — a tribute to the persistence and ability of the evil leaders.

    b.   Parables usually have one key lesson to impart.

    c.   As one interprets a parable, he must not ignore important points; also, he must not try to make all of the details mean something!

        1.   A great danger is to make "TOO MUCH" of a parable.

        2.   Small details usually are not very important.

            a.   Example: "The Prodigal Son."

            b.   "Music and dancing, "swine" and the "ring" are very unimportant.

        3.   The poignant lesson: God's continuing love for the prodigal who wakes up and comes home!

    d.   The interpretation must be easy — it may not always be easy to discover, yet once it is discovered, it is easy to understand.

    e.   Parables are not to be made first sources of doctrine. They may be used to further illustrate or confirm doctrine that is already grounded.

B.   Study Of The **Immediate Context**: Study Of The Parable.

    1.   What is the **setting** for the parable?

    2.   Some think it is a continuing discussion of the dialogue going back to 15: 1-3.

    3.   Who was Jesus addressing?

        a.   He singled out the disciples. "And he said also unto his disciples." Verse 1

b. Some conclude that He was also addressing the Pharisees because of verse 14.
    1. "And the Pharisees also, who were covetous, heard all these things: and they derided him."
    2. However, they overheard these things; that does not mean that they were directed to them.
c. Some believe the steward represents other members of the audience (Tax collectors, Pharisees) because of their dishonest practices.

C. **Meaning Of Words** Used:
    1. **Steward**
        a. He is one who manages the affairs of another's household.
        b. He is in charge of another's possessions.

    2. **"MEASURES of oil"**
        a. This is the Greek word "Βάτους".
        b. Some transliterate it "bath."
        c. A "bath" is about 8 gallons.
        d. Thus, this man owed for 800 gallons of oil.

    3. **"MEASURES of wheat"**
        a. This is the Greek word "κόρους".
        b. Some transliterate it "cor."
        c. A "cor" was about 12 bushels.
        d. Thus, this man owed for 1,200 bushels of wheat.

D. **Detailed Study Of The Parable**:

1. The steward had tremendous responsibility over the rich man's affairs; however he is wasteful (prodigal)!

   a. "Wasteful" is from the Greek word "διασκορπίζων" (diaskorpidzoon).

   b. This word means "to waste" or "to scatter."

   c. It is interesting that this parable follows "The Parable of The Prodigal Son." Lk. 15:11-32. The prodigal "wasted" or "scattered his inheritance. 15:13

   d. It should not surprise us that Jesus would talk about a wicked person in the midst of a parable to drive home a spiritual truth. He did so in Lk. 18: 1-6 in the parable about the persistent women. Even though the judge was an uncaring and unjust man, he relieved her of her mistreatment so she would "hush and leave him alone."

2. The Rich man makes an "accusation."

   a. "What is this that I hear of thee? render the account of thy stewardship; for thou canst be no longer steward." ASV

   b. The accusation here is used in the sense that there is no question of guilt. His guilt is a non-issue.

3. How does the steward react when he is told of his fate? Verse 3

   a. He objectively and quickly evaluates the situation.

      1. He reacts objectively.

      a.   He evaluates the situation.

      b.   He acknowledges the problem and his own traits.

      c.   He has the ability to judge the situation clearly.

  2. He reacts quickly.

      a.   He has a serious problem.

      b.   There's no time to waste.

  3. He reacts realistically.

      a.   My job is lost!

      b.   I have to find a solution.

b. He develops a plan and then acts on that plan. Verse 4

  1. He reacts shrewdly.

  2. He had the ability to develop an effective strategy.

  3. Realizing that he will be fired; he seeks a course of action that will both please his lord and that will elicit the favor of his creditors.

  4. He wants to be in good favor with the rich man's debtors so they will feel a sense of indebtedness to him.

  5. Thus, when he IS fired, perhaps they will reach out and help him.

  6. At least this man's actions showed a real concern about his future.

c. He quickly implemented that strategy.

  1. He called his master's debtors.

  2. He told the man who owed 100 baths of oil to quickly settle the debt by paying for 50 baths.

  3. He told the man who owed 100 cors of wheat to quickly settle the debt by paying for 80 cors.

4. WHICH actions cause this man to be called "the unjust steward" in verse 8?
    a. Those **before** the events of the parable?
    b. Those that occur **IN** the parable?
    c. This seems to be a critical matter in properly understanding the parable.
    d. The title "The Unjust Steward" seems to get students on a track of thinking that his action IN the parable are wicked.

5. How would you view his actions IN the parable?
    a. **Sinful**?
        1. "The unjust steward, who **defrauds** his master by collusion with the debtors. (Lk. 16)."[3]
        2. "'I've got it; I know what I will do!' His **dishonest purpose** was soon revealed. He would involve all the debtors in defrauding the lord, and then presume upon their charity when he needed it."[4]
        3. "This is a business venture in which the steward helped several retailers **cheat** a wholesaler with whom they traded."[5]
        4. The steward altered the accounts of all of his master's debtors. His plan was a simple one: by **falsifying the records** he figured to gain the gratitude of the debtors, so that when he was let out of his job he would be repaid by the hospitality of his friends."[6]
        5. "**What he is doing is dishonest**. He is stealing from his boss."[7]

6. Those who suggest he was being dishonest claim that he reduces the amount of debt (two examples are given) by having the debtors rewrite the bill of sale ("having sat down") therefore avoiding liability for tampering.

7. Questions about this view:
    a. Is THIS why he is called "the unjust steward?"
    b. If he was being dishonest, why did his lord "commend" him? 8
    c. Was the lord saying:
        1. I just appreciate or admire the ways of the worldly people and their shrewdness?
        2. "That's really clever!"
    d. Would you commend one who:
        1. Was cheating on a test if you were the teacher?
        2. Hired subcontractors in working on your house and defrauded them?

8. Notice who observed the steward's actions with favor and who observed them with disfavor.

People	Favorably	Unfavorably
Steward	+	
Debtors	+	
Master	+	

b. **Wise?**
   1. Was he correcting a wrong?
      a. The New Bible Commentary Revised says, "Recent study of Jewish law has suggested that the steward may not have been acting dishonestly at this point. He was merely releasing the debtors from the huge interest payments which had been imposed (quite illegally) when the loans were made to them."[8]
      b. Had his master charged "usury?" Lev. 25:36,37; Dt. 23:19
      c. Would this have caused his master to be pleased?
   2. Was he "forgiving" the interest on their debt so his master could at least have him money back?
      a. Governments do this on loans made to other countries.
      b. Banks do it sometimes too.
      c. Would this have caused his master to be pleased?
   3. Was he trying to make friends?
      a. The numbers are arbitrary (the steward simply wanted to appease and befriend the debtors).
      b. He was trying to make friends who would help him in his unemployment and inability to provide for himself.
      c. Would this have caused his master to be pleased?

4. Was he a broker for his master?
   a. Observe that both the master and the creditors praised him. It is possible these creditors were not paying the lord in a timely manner.
   b. Therefore, he may have agreed to forego his own commission (eliminated his profit) to help them lower their debt.
   c. Would this have made his master, his creditors, and the steward himself pleased?

E. What Is The **Message** Of This Parable For Jesus' Disciples?
   1. Jesus is emphasizing that His disciples can make one of two choices: will you follow God or mammon? 13

   2. Is money (mammon) inherently unrighteous? Righteous? It is neither unrighteous nor righteous.

   3. Why does Jesus speak of "unrighteous mammon?"
      a. He is emphasizing a contrast between "unrighteous mammon" and "true riches."
         1. "Unrighteous mammon" is temporal; "true riches" are eternal!
         2. Mammon is "unrighteous" because it can be used for personal emphasis (selfish interest) to the neglect or misuse of others.

a. Mt. 19:24 "And again I say unto you, It is easier for a camel to go through the eye of a needle, than for a rich man to enter into the kingdom of God."

b. I Tim. 6:10 "For the love of money is the root of all evil: which while some coveted after, they have erred from the faith, and pierced themselves through with many sorrows."

c. Enslavement to "mammon" will not help us in the judgment at all; in fact, it will destroy us! Mt. 16:26 "For what is a man profited, if he shall gain the whole world, and lose his own soul? or what shall a man give in exchange for his soul?"

d. Earthly things are SO fleeting. Mt. 6:19,20 "Lay not up for yourselves treasures upon earth, where moth and rust doth corrupt, and where thieves break through and steal: 20But lay up for yourselves treasures in heaven, where neither moth nor rust doth corrupt, and where thieves do not break through nor steal:"

b. If the Christian's focus is on "unrighteous mammon", he will be with the wicked whose focus was on "unrighteous mammon" in Hell forever.

    c.   If Christians are unfaithful in their use of their Master's wealth, He will be cast them out.

    d.   Christians must use their blessings to glorify God and to assist their fellowman, not just for selfish interests!

4.   Christians must have deep and abiding concern for their future!

    a.   Sadly, godly people oftentimes have much less concern for their plight spiritually that people of the world do for their position materially.

    b.   Many who have true riches tragically often do not exhibit much concern for their future.

    c.   Christians should be DILIGENT in the preparing for the present and future affairs of the kingdom!

        1.   Consider the time athletes spend in sports to perfect their game.

        2.   How much effort do God's people put into their spiritual lives?

        3.   Do we work harder for our earthly future or our spiritual future?

    d.   Godly people should be honest and shrewd both in material matters and in spiritual matters.

    e.   God's people should be righteous in their use of money and worldly things. They must also be righteous in their use of the godly things!

    f.   Perhaps Jesus' advice should be remembered here, "Be ye therefore wise as serpents, and harmless as doves." Mt. 10:16

V. Considerations For Personal Application:

A. Stewardship Is Expected Of God's People!

1. Elders are stewards of God's spiritual family. Tit. 1:7 "as the steward of God;"

2. Christians are to be stewards of God's gifts. I Pet. 4:10 "As every man hath received the gift, even so minister the same one to another, as good stewards of the manifold grace of God."

3. We must be faithful stewards! I Cor. 4:2 "Moreover it is required in stewards, that a man be found faithful."

4. We will all give account of our stewardship!
   a. Rom. 14:12 "So then every one of us shall give account of himself to God."
   b. II Cor. 5:10 "For we must all appear before the judgment seat of Christ; that every one may receive the things done in his body, according to that he hath done, whether it be good or bad."

B. Christians Should Have GREAT FERVENCY To Prepare For Their Future!

1. If we are only interested in this life, we should put our focus upon material gain.

2. If we are interested in our spiritual life and Heaven, we should put our focus upon proper use of things and having a proper perspective of them, and realize that our use of money and material things here is a part of what determines our eternal destiny!

Endnotes:

[1]Taylor, Robert. "Introduction Of The Savior's Parables," from *The Parables Of Our Savior*, Garfield Heights Church of Christ Second Annual Lectureship, 1983, pp. 1-13.

[2]Burton Coffman's, *Commentary On Luke*, Austin, TX: Firm Foundation Publishing House, 1975; p. 350.

[3]McClintock & Strong, *Cyclopedia of Biblical, Theological, and Ecclesiastical Literature*, Vol. IX – RH-ST; "Steward", Grand Rapids, MI: Baker Book House, p. 1020.

[4]Coffman, Ibid, p. 346.

[5]Ray Summers, *Commentary on Luke*, P. 190.

[6]Neil Lightfoot, *The Parables Of Jesus*, Part 2, p. 33

[7]Wesley Simon. WVBS Course Notes under "Parables."

[8]Guthrie, D. and Motyer, J.A. *The New Bible Commentary Revised*, Grand Rapids, MI: Erdmans Publishing Co., 1970. pp. 912,913.

ASSIGNMENT: Matthew 5:17; Ephesians 2:15

A. Study these Texts From Several Different Translations.

B. Observe The Difference In Words That Are Used In Translations.

C. Do You See A Contradiction In Some Translations?

D. Carefully Observe The Contexts Of These Scriptures To Aid Your Understanding.

Lesson Four

Translation Issues: Seeming Contradictions

Introduction:

    A.   Some Passages When Looked At Side By Side May Appear To Espouse Contradictions.

    B.   Today, We Will Look At One Pair Of Those Verses.

I.   The Scriptures:

    A.   **Matt. 5:17** "Think not that I am come to **destroy** the law, or the prophets: I am not come to **destroy**, but to fulfil."

    B.   **Eph. 2:15** "**Having abolished** in his flesh the enmity, *even* the law of commandments *contained* in ordinances; for to make in himself of twain one new man, *so* making peace;"

    C.   These Quotes Are From The KJV.

II. The Problem:

A. One Verse Seems To Suggest That Jesus Did NOT Come To Destroy The Law.

B. The Other Passage Explicitly Affirms That He DID Abolish It.

C. This Seems To Be A Contradiction.

III. Possible Interpretations Or Solutions To The Problem.

A. The Old Law Was In Effect And Still Is; Man Is Subject To It.

B. That Old Law Was Flawed And Needed To Be Replaced. God Was Making Things Up As He Went Along.

C. The Old Law Served Its Purpose; It Was Removed Or Replaced By Christ With The New Covenant.

D. These Two Verses Are Talking About Two Different Things.

IV. **Tools To Use In Solving This Problem.**
   A. **Different Translations**.

   B. The **Context Of Each Passage**.

   C. **In-depth Study Of Each Passage Including The Words That Seem To Contradict**.

   D. **Other Scriptures**.

V. **Using Our Tools To Solve The Problem.**
   A. One Tool: Study **Other Translations**:
     1. ASV
       a. Mt. 5:17 "Think not that I came to **destroy** the law or the prophets: I came not to **destroy**, but to fulfil."
       b. Eph. 2:15 "**having abolished** in the flesh the enmity, even the law of commandments contained in ordinances; that he might create in himself of the two one new man, so making peace;"

     2. NKJV
       a. Matt. 5:17 "Do not think that I have come to **destroy** the Law or the Prophets. I have not come to **destroy**, but to fulfil."
       b. Eph. 2:15 "**Having abolished** in His flesh the enmity, that is, the law of commandments contained in ordinances;

so as to create in Himself one new man from the two, thus making peace,"

3. NIV
    a. Mt. 5:17 ""Do not think that I have come to **abolish** the Law or the Prophets; I have not come to **abolish** them but to fulfill them."
    b. Eph. 2:15 "**by abolishing** in his flesh the law with its commandments and regulations. His purpose was to create in himself one new man out of the two, thus making peace,"

4. RSV
    a. Mt. 5:17 "Think not that I have come to **abolish** the law and the prophets; I have come not to **abolish** them but to fulfil them."
    b. Eph. 2:15 "**by abolishing** in his flesh the law of commandments and ordinances, that he might create in himself one new man in place of the two, so making peace,"

5. New English Bible
    a. Mt. 5:17 "Do not suppose that I have come to **abolish** the Law and the prophets; I did not come to **abolish**, but to complete."
    b. Eph. 2:15 "for he **annulled** the law with its rules and regulations, so as to create out of the two a single new humanity in himself, thereby making peace."

6. New Berkley Translation
   a. Mt. 5:17 "Do not suppose that I came to **annul** the Law or the prophets. I did not come to **abolish** but to complete them;"
   b. Eph. 2:15 "by **abolishing** the Law of commandments with its regulations, so that in Himself He might create the two into one new person and thus make peace,"

7. Moffatt's Translation
   a. Mt. 5:17 "Never imagine I have come to **destroy** the Law or the prophets; I have not come to **destroy** but to fulfil."
   b. Eph. 2:15 "in his own flesh he **put an end to** the feud of the Law with its code of commands, so as to make peace by the creation of a new Man in himself out of both parties,"

8. McCord's Translation
   a. Mt. 5:17 "Do not think I have come to **destroy** the law or the prophets. I have not come to **destroy**, but to fulfill."
   b. Eph. 2:15 "He **set aside** the law of commandments in ordinances, that he might create in himself one new man of the two, making peace;"

9. English Version For The Deaf
   a. Mt. 5:17 "Don't think that I have come to **destroy** the law of Moses or the teaching of the prophets. I have not come to **destroy** their teachings. I came to give full meaning to their teachings."

b.   Eph. 2:15 "The Jewish law had many commandments and rules. But Christ **ended** that law. Christ's purpose was to make the two groups of people (Jew and non-Jew) become one new people in him. By dong this Christ would make peace."

10. Living Bible
   a.   Mt. 5:17 "Don't misunderstand why I have come—it isn't to **cancel** the law of Moses and the warning of the prophets. No, I came to fulfill them, and to make them all come true."
   b.   Eph. 2:15 "By his death he **ended** the angry resentment between us, caused by the Jewish laws which favored the Jews and excluded the Gentiles, for he died to annul that whole system of Jewish laws. Then he took the two groups that had been opposed to each other and made them parts of himself; thus he fused us together to become one new person, and at last there was peace."

11. The Amplified Bible
   a.   Mt. 5:17 "Do not think that I have come **to do away with or undo** the Law and the prophets; I have come not **to do away with or undo**, but to complete and fulfill them."
   b.   Eph. 2:15 "By **abolishing** in His [own crucified] flesh the enmity [caused by] the Law with its decrees and ordinances—which He annulled; that He from the two might create in Himself one new man—

one new quality of humanity out of the two—so making peace."

12. Observations from using this tool:
    a. Some translations have Jesus saying He **did not come to abolish** the Law and He **DID abolish** the Law!
    b. These translations present contradictory statements.
    c. SERIOUS QUESTIONS arise:
        1. Are these two verses affirming contradictory truths about the status of the Law Of Moses?
        2. Does the Bible contradict Itself?
        3. Is it just a seeming contradiction?
    d. Using this tool may not clear up people's misunderstandings; let's take another tool from our toolbox.

B. What Is The **Context** Of Each Passage?
    1. In Matthew 5, Jesus is speaking during the Sermon on the Mount. The Law of Moses was still in effect at that time.

    2. In Ephesians 2, Paul is writing to Christians in Ephesus; the New Law is in effect.

C. **In-depth Study Of Each Passage**.
    1. Mt. 5:17
        a. "Think not"
            1. What does this imply?
            2. There is some misconception that He wants to address.

  b. What is the confusion? That He might destroy the Law of Moses.
    1. "Destroy"
    2. Greek word "καταλῦσαι"(katalusai)
    3. What does it mean? To destroy or nullify; to defeat or destroy its purpose.
    4. Other places this word is used:
      a. Ac. 5:39 "overthrow." Gamaliel speaking of Peter and John's preaching and Christianity. "But if it be of God, ye cannot **overthrow** it;"
      b. Jn. 10:35 "broken." "The scripture cannot be **broken**;"
      c. Mt. 24:2 "thrown down." Jesus talking about the destruction of the Temple and the surrounding buildings in the Fall of Jerusalem said, "There shall not be left here one stone upon another, that shall not be **thrown down**."
  c. Why might people feel this way?
    1. They saw Jesus as establishing an earthly kingdom.
    2. He would want to replace the existing system.
  d. But to "fulfil" — complete.
    1. This is an antithesis (contrasting words in a phrase)
    2. He came NOT "to destroy" BUT "to fulfill."
    3. Example: Students in college; person paying a loan. These are fulfilled

without being made invalid or destroyed.
4. His purpose was not to "start over" but to complete or fulfil what had been started.

e. Is there any significance to the Law and the Prophets?
   1. Lk. 24:44 "And he said unto them, These *are* the words which I spake unto you, while I was yet with you, that all things must be fulfilled, which were written in the law of Moses, and *in* the prophets, and *in* the psalms, concerning me."
   2. The Jews broke the O.T. into 3 parts, Law of Moses, Prophets, and Psalms.
   3. Is there any significance to "Law AND Prophets" or "Law OR Prophets?"

2. Eph. 2:15
   a. Gentile Christians are being addressed. 1:1; 2:11
   b. Paul's theme: Christ has made possible reconciliation for Jews and Gentile "in Him;" that is, "in His Church!
   c. Abolished!
      1. "καταργήσας" (katargaysas)
      2. This word means to abolish, to nullify, to void!
      3. Other passages where this word is used.
         a. Rom. 6:6 "Knowing this, that our old man is crucified with *him*, that the body of sin might

be **destroyed**, that henceforth we should not serve sin."

b. I Cor. 13:8 "Charity never faileth: but whether *there be* prophecies, they **shall fail**; whether *there be* tongues, they shall cease; whether *there be* knowledge, it shall **vanish away**."

c. I Cor. 15:24 "Then *cometh* the end, when he shall have delivered up the kingdom to God, even the Father; when he **shall have put down** all rule and all authority and power."

d. I Cor. 15:26 "The last enemy *that* shall be **destroyed** *is* death."

e. Rom. 7:6 "But now **we are delivered** from the law, that being dead wherein we were held; that we should serve in newness of spirit, and not *in* the oldness of the letter."

d. What did He abolish? The enmity. The division between Jews and Gentiles.

e. What is that enmity?

1. The "law of commandments contained in ordinances" is an "**apposition**" to the word "enmity" (It helps to further explain it.)

2. The enmity is the law of commandments contained in ordinances.

3. The word for "law" is the Greek word "δόγμασιν" (dogmasin); the

word transliterated gives us the English word "dogma."

    4.   What is this law? The whole Jewish system!

        a.   It is not just the ceremonial laws of the Mosaic system.

        b.   Rom. 7:6,7

        c.   The Law of Moses, given only to Jews, is removed so that both can be reunited under one law, the Law of Christ.

3.   Different words are used in the Greek text. There is no contradiction here at all!

D. **Evaluation Of The Possible Interpretations In Light Of Scripture:**

    1.   If the Old Law is still in effect, then all of it must be obeyed!

        a.   Mt. 5:18

        b.   Gal. 5:1-4

        c.   This would include animal sacrifice, circumcision, etc.

    2.   If the Old Law was flawed and needed to be replaced, God is not all powerful and cannot produce something that is perfect.

        a.   That Old Law did exactly what He planned it to do!

        b.   It was a schoolmaster to bring man to Christ. Gal. 3:24 "Wherefore the law was our schoolmaster to bring us unto Christ, that we might be justified by faith."

   c. God was making things up as He went along; the Law fulfilled the very purpose He had for it. Gal. 4:4 "In the fulness of time." It was not on the "spur of the moment."

 3. The Old Law served its purpose; It was removed or replace by Christ with the New Covenant.

   a. Col. 2:14 "Blotting out the handwriting of ordinances that was against us, which was contrary to us, and took it out of the way, nailing it to his cross;"

   b. It was contrary to man because sinful man could not live perfectly; that Law provided no way for complete justification with God.

   c. Gal. 3:19-25

   d. Christ is the end of the Law.

     1. Rom. 10:4 "For Christ *is* the end of the law for righteousness to every one that believeth."

     2. Rom. 7:6,7 "But now we are **delivered from** [same Greek word as in Eph. 2:15] the law, that being dead wherein we were held; that we should serve in newness of spirit, and not *in* the oldness of the letter. [7]What shall we say then? *Is* the law sin? God forbid. Nay, I had not known sin, but by the law: for I had not known lust, except the law had said, Thou shalt not covet."

   e. If these verses are discussing the same thing, the Law of Moses, one asserts that

He did not come to destroy It, the other asserts that he DID abolish It!

4. If these two verses are talking about two different things, what would it be?
   a. Matthew is speaking about Christ's relationship to It. He came to fulfill It, not destroy Its purpose.
   b. Ephesians is discussing why the Law was removed. It was removed so all could be reunited under one Law.

E. **Some Translations May Suggest A Contradiction; However, There Is Absolutely No Contradiction In These Two Verses At All!**

Suggested Study Material:
"Difficult Texts From The Gospel Accounts. Matthew 5:17; 'I Am Not Come To Destroy The Law...But To Fulfill," by W.T. Hamilton. From *Difficult Texts Of The New Testament Explained*, edited by Wendell Winkler. 1981 Forth Worth Lectures, pp. 92-95.

ASSIGNMENT: Study Of Capitalization And Lower Case Use Of Words
A. "Lamb" and "lamb"
   1. Jn. 1:29,36; Rev. 5:6; 21:22,23,27; 22:1

   2. Ac. 8:32; I Pet. 1:19

B. "Spirit" and "spirit"
    1. Gal. 5:22,25

    2. Gal. 6:1,8,18

    3. I Jn. 4:1-3

    4. Jn. 4:24

    5. Rom. 8:4,16

C. "Lord" and "lord"
    1. Jn. 13:6,9,13,14,25,36,37

    2. Jn. 13:16; Ac. 25:26; I Pet. 3:6

    3. Ac. 9:5

Translation Issues: Capitalization

I. The Problem:

A. Observe Translation Of Words When They Are Sometimes Capitalized And At Other Times They Are Not Capitalized.

B. Observe The Impact Of Seeing A Word In Upper Case And In Lower Case.
   1. When **Bond** got into trouble with the law, he had to post **bond**."

   2. "I went to **the baker's** to get a loaf of bread."
      "I went to **the Baker's** to get a loaf of bread."

C. Question: How Does Capitalization Affect Your Response To What You Are Reading?
   1. Immediately you may think that the word refers to a person.

   2. Caution: BE CAREFUL THAT YOU DO NOT STOP THINKING!

D. Two Examples Of Bible Words In Lower Case And In Capitals.
   1. "**Lord**"
      a. Caps:

1. Mt. 7:21,22 "**Lord, Lord**"
2. Jn. 20:28 "My **Lord** and my God"
3. Ac. 9:5 "Who art thou, **Lord**?"
4. Eph. 1:3 "Blessed be the God and Father of our **Lord** Jesus Christ..."

b. Lower case:
   1. Mt. 18:27 "The **lord** of that servant"
   2. Mt. 20:8 "the **lord** of the vineyard"
   3. Jn. 13:16 "The servant is not greater than his **lord**;"

c. Why is the word "lord" often capitalized and at other times it is not capitalized?

2. **"God"**
   a. It is never capitalized in the Nestle's Greek text.
   b. However, nearly every time it is capitalized when translated.
   c. 3 times it is translated "**god**."
      1. Ac. 12:22 "And the people gave a shout, saying, It is the voice of a **god**, and not of a man."
      2. Ac. 28:6 "Howbeit they looked when he should have swollen, or fallen down dead suddenly: but after they had looked a great while, and saw no harm come to him, they changed their minds, and said that he was a **god**."
      3. II Cor. 4:4 "In whom the **god** of this world hath blinded the minds of them which believe not, lest the light of the glorious gospel of Christ, who is the image of God, should shine unto them."

a. In a Bible class, one brother asked, "Who IS this "god of this world? Is it REALLY Satan?"

b. Everyone immediately said, "Yes!"

c. He's the only one who wants to take Truth out of the hearts of believers.

d. He's the only one who veils the Truth.

e. One brother immediately spoke up and said, "It CAN'T be referring to God because "god" is a little "g."

f. Almost every commentary will affirm that this is referring to Satan.

g. He's called "the prince of this world" and "prince of the power of the air."

h. Jn. 12:31; 14:30; Eph. 2:2

i. Observations:

1. Does this HAVE to refer to Satan?

2. "God" is used 5 times in II Cor. 4; it is the same word every time! "θεου" (theou) or "θεός (theos)." It is always lower case!

3. The passages in John 12 and 14 state the Satan is "prince of this world." "World" is the word "κόσμος" (kosmos) meaning "the created world."

4. II Cor. 4 uses the word "τους αἰῶνος τούτου" (tous aioonos toutou) meaning "this age."

5. Does God ever "harden people's hearts?"
   a. What about Pharaoh?
   b. What about II Thess. 2:11,12 "And for this cause God shall send them strong delusion, that they should believe a lie: That they all might be damned who believed not the truth, but had pleasure in unrighteousness."
   g. Barnes says that some of the "church fathers" and Adam Clarke believed that this referred to the true God. [1]

E. Information About Biblical Capitalization!
   1. Manuscripts of the N.T. are of two types: [2]
      a. Uncials — these manuscripts are written in ALL capitalization!
         1. There are about 375 of these manuscripts in existence.
            a. About 90 are written on papyri (thin strips of papyrus plant laid side by side and formed into a sheet).
            b. About 250 are on vellum (parchment).

    c.   About 30 are on broken pieces of pottery called ostraca.

2.   These manuscripts were in all large letters, there was no space between words; there was no punctuation!

3.   Examples of how an English text would appear if written as uncials:

    a.   John 1:1-3:

INTHEBEGINNINGWASTHEW
ORDANDTHEWORDWASWI
THGODANDTHEWORDWAS
GODTHESAMEWASINTHE
BEGINNINGWITHGODALL
THINGSWEREMADEBYHIM
ANDWITHOUTHIMWASNOT
ANYTHINGMADETHATWAS
MADE.

    b.   Of Rom. 1:1,2:

PAULASERVANTOFJESUS
CHRISTCALLEDTOBEAN
APOSTLESEPARATEDUNTO
THEGOSPELOFGODWHICH
HEHADPROMISEDAFOREBY
HISPROPHETSINTHEHOLY
SCRIPTURES.

4.   The following picture is of a Greek uncial codex, Papyrus 66, John 1:1-14:

5. These documents were often written in columns as seen in the following picture of John 1 from Codex Sinaiticus (01).

b. Cursives — these manuscripts are written in a running hand-style; handwritten. They are first seen in the 9th Century!

2. Manuscripts of the O.T.
   a. All the letters are consonants; there are NO vowels!
   b. "Jehovah" is "YHWH."
   c. The Hebrew was written from right to left.

d. The following picture is of a Hebrew manuscript from the Dead Sea Scrolls:

e. The Massoretes, scribes who lived at Tiberias, began to put vowels and accents into the Hebrew text to give consistency.[3]

3. SO who decided which words should be in lower case and which words should be capitalized in the texts?
   a. Translators have capitalized proper names and words that they believe refer to Deity, et. al.
   b. The concern about this is that one's theology may have great influence in some words that the translator capitalizes and some words that he places in lower case.

F. Comparison Of The Nestle Greek Text And The King James Version.
   1. Some passages or parts of passages are in ALL caps in the Nestle Greek Text and in English translations. Mt. 27:37; Mk. 15:26; Lk. 23:38; Jn. 19:19; Ac. 17:23; Rev. 17:5; Rev. 19:16.

2. One word is in ALL caps in the English text (KJV) but is NOT in the Nestle Greek Text. It Is Mt. 1:21 "JESUS."

3. Certain types of words are ALWAYS capitalized in both the Greek and the English texts.
   a. They are words that begin sentences and those that proper nouns (names of people) and places.
   b. People: Joseph, Mary, John; Pharisees and Sadducees.
   c. Places: Egypt, Galilee.

4. Some words are capitalized at times in the Nestle's Greek text; sometimes they are not.
   a. "Christ"
      1. It is ALWAYS capitalized in the Nestle Greek text in Romans, I Corinthians, II Corinthians, Galatians, Ephesians, Philippians, Colossians, Titus, Philemon, Hebrews, James, II Peter, II John, and Jude.
      2. It is ALWAYS capitalized when used in "Jesus Christ."
      3. It is NOT capitalized in Mt. 2:4; 16:17,20; Mk. 8:29; 12:35 Ac. 2:36 and many other places.
      4. It is NEVER capitalized in Luke and John.
   b. "Father"
      1. It is USUALLY in the lower case in the Nestle Greek text.
      2. It IS capitalized in Mt. 6:9; Lk. 11:2.

3. It, like other words, is capitalized as the first word in an address.

5. Many words are capitalized in the English translations that are not capitalized in the original language. The following are a sample:
   a. "Apostle" Heb. 3:1
   b. "Baptist" Mt. 3:1; Mk. 6:14
   c. "Comforter" Jn. 14:16,26; 15:26; 16:7
   d. "God." It is NEVER capitalized in Nestle's Greek text!
   e. "Holy Ghost" Mt. 1:20; 3:11
   f. "Lord." It is always small case in the Nestle Greek text.
   g. "Passover." Lk. 22:1
   h. "Pentecost." Ac. 2:1; 20:16
   i. "Satan" (Except in Rev. 12:9; 20:2; "Satan's" in 2:13)

G. Different translations capitalize different words.
   1. Introduction of the NKJV: "Readers of the Authorized Version will immediately be struck by the absence of several pronouns: *thee, thou,* and *ye* are replaced by the simple *you,* while *your* and *yours* are substituted for *thy* and *thine* as applicable. *Thee, thou, thy,* and *thine* were once forms of address to express a special relationship to human as well as divine persons. These pronouns are no longer part of our language. However, reverence for God in the present work is preserved by capitalizing pronouns, including *You, Your,* and *Yours,* which refer to Him." [4]

2. Translations make arbitrary choices about capitalizing different words. Example: Mt. 3:14-17

   a. In the Nestle's Greek text, only "John" and "Jesus" (twice) are capitalized.

   b. KJV: "But **John** forbad him, saying, **I** have need to be baptized of thee, and comest thou to me? And **Jesus** answering said unto him, Suffer it to be so now: for thus it becometh us to fulfil all righteousness. Then he suffered him. And **Jesus**, when he was baptized, went up straightway out of the water: and, lo, the heavens were opened unto him, and he saw the **Spirit** of **God** descending like a dove, and lighting upon him: And lo a voice from heaven, saying, This is my beloved **Son**, in whom **I** am well pleased."

   c. ASV: "But **John** would have hindered him, saying, **I** have need to be baptized of thee, and comest thou to me? But **Jesus** answering said unto him, Suffer it now: for thus it becometh us to fulfil all righteousness. Then he suffereth him. And **Jesus** when he was baptized, went up straightway from the water: and lo, the heavens were opened unto him, and he saw the **Spirit** of **God** descending as a dove, and coming upon him; and lo, a voice out of the heavens, saying, This is my beloved **Son**, in whom **I** am well pleased."

   d. NIV: "But **John** tried to deter him, saying, 'I need to be baptized by you, and do you come to me?' **Jesus** replied, 'Let it be so now; it is proper for us to do this to fulfill all righteousness.' Then **John** consented. As soon as **Jesus** was baptized, he went up out of the water. At that moment heaven was opened, and he saw the **Spirit** of **God** descending like a dove and lighting on him. And a voice from heaven said, '**This** is my **Son**, whom I love; with him I am well pleased.'"

e. NKJV: "But **John** tried to prevent **Him**, saying, 'I have need to be baptized by **You**, and are **You** coming to me?' And **Jesus** answered and said to him, 'Permit it to be so now, for thus it is fitting for us to fulfill all righteousness.' Then he allowed **Him**. And **Jesus**, when **He** had been baptized, came up immediately from the water; and behold, the heavens were opened to **Him**, and **He** saw the **Spirit** of **God** descending like a dove and alighting upon **Him**. And suddenly a voice came from heaven, saying, 'This is **My** beloved **Son**, in whom I am well-pleased.'"

II. Possible Interpretations Or Solutions To The Problem:
A. "**Lamb**": To What May It Refer?
1. It may refer to Jesus.

2. It may refer to a sheep.

B. **"Lord"**: To What May It Refer?
   1. It may refer to Jesus.

   2. It may refer to a master.

C. **"Spirit"**
   1. It may refer to the Holy Spirit.

   2. It may refer to a demon.

   3. It may refer to a person's heart or attitude.

III. **Tools To Use In Solving This Problem:**
   A. **Different Translations.**

   B. **Context, Context, Context!**

IV. **Using Our Tools To Solve This Problem.**
   A. **"Lamb"**
      1. Caps:
         a. Jn. 1:29,36; Rev. 5:6; 21:22,23,27; 22:1
         b. In each of these passages, "Lamb" refers to Jesus Christ;" thus, it is capitalized by the translators.

      2. Lower case:
         a. Passages:
            1. Jn. 21:15 "Feed my **lambs**."
            2. Ac. 8:32 "like a **lamb** dumb before

his shearer, so opened he not his mouth:"

3. I Pet. 1:19 "But with the precious blood of Christ, as of a **lamb** without blemish and without spot:"

4. Rev. 13:11 "And I beheld another beast coming up out of the earth; and he had two horns like a **lamb**, and he spake as a dragon."

b. The first passage refers to the Christians; they are his "lambs" or "sheep" who hear His voice and follow Him.

c. The last three of these passages use "lamb" as a simile. The first two describe Jesus as a lamb, however, they are not calling Him "the Lamb."

B "**Lord**"
1. Caps:
   a. Passages:
      1. Mt. 7:21,22 "**Lord, Lord**"
      2. Jn. 20:28 "My **Lord** and my God"
      3. Ac. 9:5 "Who art thou, **Lord**?"
      4. Eph. 1:3 "Blessed by the God and Father of our **Lord** Jesus Christ..."
      5. Jn. 13:6,9,13,25,36,37
   b. All of these passages refer to Jesus.

2. Lower case:
   a. Passages:
      1. Mt. 18:27 "The **lord** of that servant"
      2. Mt. 20:8 "the **lord** of the vineyard"
      3. Jn. 13:16 "The servant is not greater than his **lord**;"

4. Ac. 25:26 "I have no certain thing to write unto my **lord**."

5. I Pet. 3:6 "Sarah obeyed Abraham, calling him **lord**:"

b. These passages refer to masters or those in authority in general.

C. **"Spirit"**

1. Lower case:
   a. "Unclean **spirit**" Mt. 12:43; Mk. 1:23,26; 3:30; 5:2,8
   b. "Poor in **spirit**" Mt. 5:3
   c. Gal. 6:1 "**spirit** of meekness."
   d. Gal. 6:18 "your **spirit**."

2. Upper case:
   a. "The **Spirit** said unto Philip" Ac. 8:29
   b. "The **Spirit** said unto him" Ac. 10:19
   c. "The **Spirit** bade me go with them" Ac. 11:12

3. Both cases:
   a. I Cor. 2:11 "For what man knoweth the things of a man, save the **spirit of man** which is in him? even so the things of God knoweth no man, but the **Spirit of God**."
   b. Gal. 5:22,25 "**Spirit**"; 6:1 "**spirit** of meekness"; 6:8 "**Spirit**"; 6:18 "your **spirit**."

4. Passages illustrating the translation difficulties.
   a. When you see "Spirit," how would you typically interpret it? "Holy Spirit."

b. John 4:24 "God is **a Spirit**: and they that worship him must worship him in spirit and in truth."

    1. If we are consistent, why wouldn't we say that "God is the Holy Spirit?"

    2. The Greek literally says, "God is spirit."

c. Rom. 8:4 "who walk not after the flesh, but after the **Spirit**."

    1. How would you interpret these phrases just by observation?

    2. What does this translation suggest?

        a. The contrast of the flesh ruling compare to the Holy Spirit ruling in one's life.

        b. What if "Spirit" were "spirit?" It would contrast one putting his focus upon the flesh (giving in to the struggles with the body and temptation) compared to one putting his focus upon the spiritual things (his real being and his eternal destiny).

d. Rom. 8:15 "For ye have not received the **spirit** of bondage again to fear; but ye have received the **Spirit** of adoption, whereby we cry, Abba, Father."

    1. How would you interpret these phrases just by observation?

        a. "spirit of bondage" — frame of mind or principle of slavery.

        b. "Spirit of adoption" — Holy Spirit of adoption. Because Christians receive the Holy

Spirit, they are adopted children of God.

2. Why could this not be contrasting the principle of slavery with the principle of adoption, sonship, and peace.

e. Gal. 5:19,22

   1. "Now the works of the **flesh** are manifest, which are these;.... But the **fruit of the Spirit** is"

   2. What does this translation suggest?

      a. The contrast of the flesh ruling compare to the Holy Spirit ruling in one's life.

      b. What if "Spirit" were "spirit?" It would contrast one putting his focus upon the flesh (giving in to the struggles with the body and temptation) compared to one putting his focus upon the spiritual things (his real being and his eternal destiny).

   3. Observe verse 19 in the NIV: "The acts of the **sinful nature** are obvious:"

      a. The Greek phrase is "τὰ ἔργα τῆς σαρκός" (ta erga tays sarkos).

      b. It should be translated "the works of the flesh."

      c. There is NO justification to translate "σαρκός" (sarkos) as "sinful nature."

      d. It comes from a Calvinistic perspective.

1. This view suggests that He directly impacts one's heart.
2. It affirms that the Holy Spirit instantaneously transforms the sinner's heart without man's desire or help.

f. I Jn. 4:1-3 "Beloved, believe not every **spirit**, but try the **spirits** whether they are of God: because many false prophets are gone out into the world. Hereby know ye the **Spirit** of God: Every **spirit** that confesseth that Jesus Christ is come in the flesh is of God: And every **spirit** that confesseth not that Jesus Christ is come in the flesh is not of God: and this is that **spirit** of antichrist, whereof ye have heard that it should come; and even now already is it in the world."

1. "spirits" refers to those who teach.
2. "spirit" is used of those who deny God's Truths.
3. What does "Spirit of God" imply? The Holy Spirit.
4. Why could this not be contrasting those who deny God with those who believe and teach Truth?
5. Verse 6 discusses the "the **spirit of truth**, and the **spirit of error**."

II. The Application.
A. Before Coming To A Concrete Interpretation, THINK! Do Not Jump To A Conclusion Just Because A Word Is Capitalized In A Translation.

B. Brethren Need To Be Respectful To One Another If They Disagree About The Interpretation Of A Word; About **Who** Or To **What** It Has Reference.

C. Consider Other's Suggestions.

D. It Is So Easy To Become Angry, Judgmental, And To Draw Lines If One Sees A Passage Differently.
   1. Please be careful.

   2. Be slow to accuse one of advocating error.

   3. Ask yourself, "Is he seriously trying to be contextual?"

Endnotes:

[1]Barnes, Albert. *Barnes Notes On The New Testament*, Grand Rapids, MI, Kregel Publications, 1976, p. 835.

[2]Lightfoot, Neil R. *How We Got The Bible*, Second Edition. Grand Rapids, MI, Baker Book House, 1988, pp. 36-39.

[3]Ibid, pp. 90-93.

[4]The New King James Bible. Nashville, TN, Thomas Nelson, Inc., 1979 p. iv.

Assignment:
   A. Scriptures: I John 3:6,9; 5:18

B.   What Is The Problem?

C.   Possible Interpretations.

D.   Study The Context:
   1.   What are the issues John is addressing?

   2.   Study these verses in the context of I John
        and in the context of the whole Bible context.

E.   Study Different Translations.

Translation Issues: "Cannot Sin"

I. Scriptures: (KJV)

A. **I John 3:6** "Whosoever abideth in him sinneth not: whosoever sinneth hath not seen him, neither known him."

B. **I John 3:9** "Whosoever is born of God doth not commit sin; for his seed remaineth in him: and he cannot sin, because he is born of God."

C. **I John 5:18** "We know that whosoever is born of God sinneth not; but he that is begotten of God keepeth himself, and that wicked one toucheth him not."

II. The Problem:

A. These Verses Seem To Indicate That A Christian Cannot And Does Not Sin.

B. The Struggle For Students:
1. This doesn't feel right, sound right, or seem anything like the rest of the Bible.

2. Some students may feel like giving up or feel that there is no hope for them.

III. Possible Interpretations Or Solutions To The Problem.

A. Once A Person Becomes A Christian, He Cannot Sin!

B. One Who Becomes A Christian Will Always Be Saved!

C. Christians Must Either **Aspire To** Perfection, Or Must **Be** Perfect, Or They M**ust Become** Perfect!

D. If A Christian Sins, He NEVER WAS A Christian.

E. If A Christian Sins, He Is Not A Christian.

F. A Devout Christian Is One Who Stops Living A Life Of Sin Because Of The Fundamental Change That Has Occurred In Him Through True Commitment To Christ and His Will.

IV. Tools To Use To Solve This Problem:

A. **Translations**.

B. **Greek Text And Translation**.

C. **The Context Of I John**.

D. **Other Scriptures**.

E. **The Purpose of I John Being Written**.

V. **Using Our Tools To Solve This Problem**.
   A. **Translations**.
      1. Study of different translations:
         a. I John 3:6
            1. NJKV "Whoever abides in Him does not sin. Whoever sins has neither seen Him nor known Him."
            2. ASV "Whosoever abideth in him **sinneth not**: whosoever **sinneth** hath not seen him, neither knoweth him."
            3. RSV "No one who abides in him **sins**; no one who **sins** has either seen him or known him."
            4. NIV "No one who lives in him **keeps on sinning**. No one who **continues to sin** has either seen him or known him."
         b. I John 3:9
            1. NKJV "Whoever has been born of God does not practice sin; for His seed remains in him: and he cannot sin, because he has been born of God."
            2. ASV "Whosoever is begotten of God **doeth no sin**, because his seed abideth in him: and he **cannot sin**, because he is begotten of God."

3. RSV "No one born of God **commits sin**; for God's nature abides in him, and he **cannot sin** because he is born of God." (In a footnote: "This verse has been taken by some to mean that believers cannot sin. But 1:9 already reveals that believers do sin, and it outlines the method by which cleansing may be obtained. From the Greek tenses used here in 3:9 the verse might well be paraphrased, 'Whoever is born of God does not make sin the *practice* of his life.' So while believers do sin, it is not their common custom nor are they confirmed in the direction of sin, for **their nature is no longer the old, sinful nature**, but one given by God. The thought is expressed further in 5:18: a child of God does not live a life of sin because the Son of God keeps him."

4. NIV "No one who is born of God **will continue to sin**, because God's seed remains in him; he cannot **go on sinning**, because he has been born of God."

c. I John 5:18
1. NKJV "We know that whoever is born of God **does not sin**; but he that has been born of God keeps himself, and the wicked one does not touch him."
2. ASV "We know that whosoever is begotten of God **sinneth not**; but he

that was begotten of God keepeth himself, and the evil one toucheth him not."

3. RSV "We know that any one born of God **does not sin**, but He who was born of God keeps him, and the evil one does not touch him." (in a footnote: "The intention of John here would be better understood by translating this verse, "any one born of God does not keep on sinning.")

4. NIV "We know that anyone born of God **does not continue to sin**; the one who was born of God keeps him safe, and the evil one cannot harm him."

B. **Greek Text And Translation**.
   1. Translation of the difficult Scriptures:
      a. I John 3:6
         1. "οὐχ ἁμαρτάνει" (ouch hamartanei)
         2. "sins not"
         3. Declension: present tense, active voice, indicative mood, singular person.
         4. The present tense is often used in the "durative" sense suggesting continual action.
         5. Aorist tense is point action in the past; in the subjunctive mood, the second aorist denotes point action that may occur.
         6. The best translation would be "does not continue to sin."

b. I John 3:9
 1. "ἀμαρτίαν οὐ ποιεῖ" (hamartian ou poiei)
   a. "does not sin."
   b. "Does" is a present tense, active voice, indicative mood, singular person verb.
   c. The best translation would be "does not keep on doing sin."
 2. "οὐ δύναται ἀμαρτάνειν" (ou dunatai hamartanein)
   a. "is not able to sin."
   b. "Able" is a present tense, indicate mood, singular person verb.
   c. The best translation would be "is not able to keep on sinning."
c. I John 5:18 "οὐχ ἁμαρτάνει" (ouch hamartanei)
 1. "sins not"
 2. Declension: present tense, active voice, indicative mood, singular person.
 3. The best translation would be "does not continue to sin."

2. Translation of other passages within the book of I John.
 a. Another passage in I John addresses individual acts of sin.
 b. I John 2:1 "My little children, these things write I unto you, that ye **sin not**. And if any man **sin**, we have an advocate with the Father, Jesus Christ the righteous:"

    c.   Greek words:
        1.   "μὴ ἁμάρτητε" (may hamartayte)
            a.   "sin not"
            b.   Declension: Second aorist tense, active voice, subjunctive mood, singular person.
            c.   The best translation would be, "that you may not sin (commit a specific act of sin)."
        2.   "ἐάν τις ἁμάρτῃ" (ean tis hamartay)
            a.   "If anyone sins"
            b.   Declension: Second aorist tense, active voice, subjunctive mood, singular person.
            b.   The best translation would be, "if anyone sins (commits a specific act of sin)."

    3.   Proper translation does not suggest that a Christian will never sin; rather, it affirms that a Christian will not continue in a pattern of sinful living.

C. The Context Of I John.
    1.   There is a serious problem is one interprets our texts in the following ways:
        a.   Once a person becomes a Christian, he cannot sin!
        b.   If a Christian sins, he never was a Christian.
        c.   If a Christian sins, he is not a Christian.

    2.   Those interpretations contradict other passages in I John and we KNOW the Bible

does not contradict itself, either in an individual book or in the books collectively!

3. **Scriptures in I John that would contradict the "Christian must be or become sinless" interpretation:**

   a. I Jn. 1:8 "If we say that we have no sin, we deceive ourselves, and the truth is not in us." We CANNOT deny that we commit acts of sin.

   b. I Jn. 1:9 "If we confess our sins, he is faithful and just to forgive us our sins, and to cleanse us from all unrighteousness." God has provided a way whereby we can be forgiven when we DO sin!

   c. I Jn. 1:10 "If we say that we have not sinned, we make him a liar, and his word is not in us." Christians cannot deny that they sinned in the past.

   d. I Jn. 2:1 "My little children, these things write I unto you, that ye sin not. And if any man sin, we have an advocate with the Father, Jesus Christ the righteous." Although God would like for the Christian to avoid individual acts of sin, He knows that we will sin. Therefore, He has provided a say of forgiveness.

   e. I Jn. 2:2 "And he is the propitiation for our sins: and not for ours only, but also for the sins of the whole world." Christ is the appeasement for Christians when they sin.

    f.   I Jn. 5:16 "If any man see his brother sin a sin which is not unto death, he shall ask, and he shall give him life for them that sin not unto death. There is a sin unto death: I do not say that he shall pray for it."

D. **Other Scriptures** That Would Contradict "The Christian Must Be Or Become Sinless" Interpretation:
1. Rom. 6:1,2 "What shall we say then? Shall we continue in sin, that grace may abound? God forbid. How shall we, that are dead to sin, live any longer therein?"
   a. The Greek phrase here is "ἐπιμένωμεν τῇ ἁμαρτίᾳ". (epimenoomen tay hamartia)
   b. "ἐπιμένωμεν" is a present tense, subjunctive mood, plural Greek verb. It is translated "May we continue".
   c. "τῇ ἁμαρτίᾳ" is a dative phrase meaning "in sin."
   d. So the whole phrase should be translated, "May we continue in sin?"

2. Rom. 6:12 "Let not sin therefore reign in your mortal body, that ye should obey it in the lusts thereof."

3. Gal. 6:1 "Brethren, if a man be overtaken in a fault, ye which are spiritual, restore such an one in the spirit of meekness; considering thyself, lest thou also be tempted."

4. Heb. 10:26 "For if we sin wilfully after that we have received the knowledge of the truth, there remaineth no more sacrifice for sins,"

5. Js. 5:16 "Confess your faults one to another, and pray one for another, that ye may be healed. The effectual fervent prayer of a righteous man availeth much."

6. Js. 5:19,20 "Brethren, if any of you do err from the truth, and one convert him; Let him know, that he which converteth the sinner from the error of his way shall save a soul from death, and shall hide a multitude of sins."

7. Examples of the godly sinning and being forgiven:
   a. Peter, an Apostle, sinned and was forgiven.
      1. Even though he was so confident, Jesus told him he would deny Him. Mt. 26:33-35
      2. He did! Mt. 26:69-75
      3. Jesus forgave him; restored his broken confidence. Jn. 21:15-19
      4. Later, Peter showed inconsistency by eating with Gentiles, thus showing his acceptance of and fellowship with them; later when some of his Jewish brethren came, he would not eat with the Gentile brethren. Paul condemned his inconsistency! Gal. 2:11-1

    b.   Simon the sorcerer sinned and was forgiven. Ac. 8:18-24

    c.   The Parable of the Prodigal Son proclaims that God's people can sin, repent, and be forgiven. Lk. 15:11-32

E. **The Purpose Of I John Being Written.**
1. The root problem that John is addressing is Gnosticism.

2. It claimed some "special secret knowledge" for only a select few, the "pneumatic" or "spiritual."

3. Their beliefs:
    a.   The body is sinful by nature but the soul is pure.
    b.   The soul cannot be affected by what is done in the body.
    c.   Therefore, it does not matter if the body is involved in sin.

4. It denied that Christ could have possibly come in the flesh. They could not imagine Deity living in sinful flesh!

F. The Affirmations Of John In I John 3-5:
1. Becoming a Christian demands removing yourself from a sinful life.

2. One cannot be a part of God and CONTINUE to live in sin. The two cannot go together; they are in opposition to each other.

V. Evaluation Of The Possible Interpretations Or Solutions To The Problem.

A. Once A Person Becomes A Christian, He Cannot Sin!

1. God pointedly declares that Christians do and will sin.

2. Christ is the Christian's continual Advocate and Atonement.

B. One Who Becomes A Christian Will Always Be Saved!

1. The Bible clearly declares that one can leave Christ.

2. II Pet. 2:20-22; Heb. 6:4-6

C. Christians Must Aspire To Perfection, Or Must Be Perfect; Or They Must Become Perfect!

1. God reminds us that we do and will sin.

2. He did not demand perfection; He requires faithfulness.

D. If A Christian Sins, He NEVER WAS A Christian.

1. This is a false conclusion.

2. The Apostle Peter sinned; he had become a Christian; Simon the sorcerer could repent after becoming a Christian; Christians today sin and can repent also.

E. If A Christian Sins, He Is Not A Christian.
   1. This is another false conclusion.

   2. The Apostle Peter sinned; he still was a Christian; Simon the sorcerer could repent after becoming a Christian; Christians today sin and can repent also.

   3. John has affirmed in I John that Christians DO sin!

F. A Devout Christian Is One Who Stops Living A Life Of Sin Because Of The Fundamental Change That Has Occurred In Him Through True Commitment To Christ and His Will.
   1. This view is totally consistent with the teaching of I John and of the rest of the New Testament.

   2. Although Christians do occasionally sin, they cannot return to a life of sin!

VI. One Other Question From Our Text. What Is The "Seed?" I John 3:9
   A. It May Be "**His Word**."
      1. I Jn. 1:10 "If we say that we have not sinned, we make him a liar, and his **word** is not in us."

      2. I Jn. 2:5 "But whoso keepeth his **word**, in him verily is the love of God perfected: hereby know we that we are in him."

3. I Jn. 2:14 "I have written unto you, fathers, because ye have known him that is from the beginning. I have written unto you, young men, because ye are strong, and the **word of God** abideth in you, and ye have overcome the wicked one."

4. I Pet. 1:23 "Being born again, not of corruptible seed, but of incorruptible, by the **word of God**, which liveth and abideth for ever."

5. Js. 1:18 "Of his own will begat he us with the **word of truth**, that we should be a kind of firstfruits of his creatures."

6. Lk. 8:11 "**The seed is the word of God.**"
   a. The Greek word in this text is "σπόρος" (sporos).
   b. Transliterated, this is the English word "spore."
   c. This word is used to describe the "seed" in the "Parable of The Soils," in Lk. 8:5,11.
   d. The same Greek word is used in:
      1. Mk. 4:26,27 where sowing "**seed**" is discussed.
      2. I Pet. 1:23 "Being born again, not of corruptible **seed**, but of incorruptible, by the word of God, which liveth and abideth for ever."
   e. Sometimes the Greek word "σπέρμα" (sperma) is used to describe seeds that are sown.
      1. Mt. 13:24,27

      2.   Mk. 4:31 The grain of mustard seed is smaller than all **seeds**.

B. It Could Refer To Christians Allowing His Seed **(Life)** To Remain In Us!
    1.   The Greek word in I John 3:9 is "σπέρμα" (sperma).

    2.   Transliterated this is the English word "sperm."

    3.   Usage of "σπέρμα" (sperma):
        a.   All seeds have different bodies. I Cor. 15:38 "But God giveth it a body as it hath pleased him, and to **every seed** his own body."
        b.   A brother was to raise up "seed" to his childless, deceased brother under the O.T. Law of Levirate Marriage.
            1.   Mt. 22:24 "Saying, Master, Moses said, If a man die, having no children, his brother shall marry his wife, and raise up **seed** unto his brother."
            2.   The same word for "seed" is used to discuss this concept in Mk. 12:19,20,21,22 and in Lk. 20:28.
        c.   **"Abraham's seed."**
            1.   Isaac:
                a.   Heb. 11:11 "Through faith also Sarah herself received strength to conceive **seed**, and was delivered of a child when she was past age, because she

judged him faithful who had promised."

b. Heb. 11:18 "Of whom it was said, That **in Isaac shall thy seed be called:**"

2. The Jewish people:

a. Lk. 1:55 "As he spake to our fathers, to Abraham, and to **his seed** for ever."

b. Ac. 7:5,6 "And he gave him none inheritance in it, no, not *so much as* to set his foot on: yet he promised that he would give it to him for a possession, and to his **seed** after him, when *as yet* he had no child. ⁶And God spake on this wise, That his **seed** should sojourn in a strange land; and that they should bring them into bondage, and entreat *them* evil four hundred years."

c. Rom. 4:13 "For the promise, that he should be the heir of the world, *was* **not to Abraham, or to his seed**, through the law, but through the righteousness of faith."

d. Rom. 4:18 "Who against hope believed in hope, that he might become the father of many nations, according to that which was spoken, **So shall thy seed be.**"

e. Rom. 9:29 "And as Esaias said before, Except the Lord of Sabaoth had left us a **seed**, we had been as Sodom, and been made like unto Gomorrha."

3. The First Century Jews prided themselves that they were "Abraham's seed."

    a. Jn. 8:33 "They answered him, **We be Abraham's seed,** and were never in bondage to any man: how sayest thou, Ye shall be made free?"

    b. Jn. 8:37 "I know that **ye are Abraham's seed;** but ye seek to kill me, because my word hath no place in you."

4. Paul was of "Abraham's seed."

    a. "I say then, Hath God cast away his people? God forbid. For I also am an Israelite, of the **seed of Abraham,** *of* the tribe of Benjamin." Rom. 11:1

    b. II Cor. 11:22 "Are they Hebrews? so *am* I. Are they Israelites? so *am* I. Are they the **seed of Abraham**? so *am* I."

5. Christ is the "seed of Abraham."

    a. Ac. 3:25 "Ye are the children of the prophets, and of the covenant which God made with our fathers, saying unto Abraham, **And in thy seed shall all the kindreds of the earth be blessed.**"

    b. Gal. 3:16 "Now to Abraham and **his seed** were the promises made. He saith not, And to seeds, as of many; but as of one, And to thy seed, which is Christ."

c. Gal. 3:19 "Wherefore then *serveth* the law? It was added because of transgressions, **till the seed should come** to whom the promise was made; *and it was* ordained by angels in the hand of a mediator."

d. Christ took on him the seed of Abraham. He was conceived. Heb. 2:16 "For verily he took not on *him the nature of* angels; but **he took on** *him* **the seed of Abraham**."

6. People of faith, Christians are "Abraham's seed."

a. Rom. 4:16 "Therefore *it is* of faith, that *it might be* by grace; to the end the promise might be sure **to all the seed;** not to that only which is of the law, but to that also which is of the faith of Abraham; who is the father of us all,"

b. Rom. 9:7,8 "Neither, because they are the **seed of Abraham,** *are they* all children: but, In Isaac shall **thy seed** be called. [8]That is, They which are the children of the flesh, these *are* not the children of God: but the children of the promise are counted for **the seed.**"

      c.   Gal. 3:29 "And if ye *be* Christ's, then are ye **Abraham's seed**, and heirs according to the promise."

      d.   Rev. 12:17 "And the dragon was wroth with the woman, and went to make war with the **remnant of her seed**, which keep the commandments of God, and have the testimony of Jesus Christ."

  d. "Seed of David."

      1.   Jn. 7:42 "Hath not the scripture said, That Christ cometh of the **seed of David**, and out of the town of Bethlehem, where David was?"

      2.   Ac. 13:23 "Of **this man's seed** hath God according to *his* promise raised unto Israel a Saviour, Jesus:"

      3.   Rom. 1:3 "Concerning his Son Jesus Christ our Lord, which was made of the **seed of David** according to the flesh;"

      4.   II Tim. 2:8 "Remember that Jesus Christ of the **seed of David** was raised from the dead according to my gospel:"

4.   Both "σπέρμα" (sperma) and "σπόρος" (sporos) are used in II Cor. 9:10 "Now he that ministereth **seed** "σπέρμα" (sperma) to the sower both minister bread for *your* food, and multiply your **seed** [the accusative "σπόρον" (sporon) from "σπόρος" (sporos)] sown, and increase the fruits of your righteousness;)"

5. This answer is consistent with the message of I John: Christians have life "in Christ!"
   a. He was manifested to show unto us **eternal life**. I Jn. 1:2
   b. He has promised us **eternal life**. I Jn. 2:25
   c. Christians have passed from death **unto life!** I Jn. 3:14
   d. I Jn. 5:11,12 "And this is the record, that God hath given to us **eternal life**, and this life is in his Son. He that hath the Son hath life;"
   e. The purpose of the book of I John "These things have I written unto you that believe on the name of the Son of God; that ye may know that ye have **eternal life**, and that ye may believe on the name of the Son of God." I Jn. 5:13

Assignment:
   A. Study I Cor. 7:12-24.

   B. In Particular, What Do These Two Specific Verses Mean:
      1. I Cor 7:15 "Not under bondage?"

      2. I Cor. 7:20,24 "Abide in the calling wherein you were called?"

   C. What Are Possible Interpretations Of These Texts?

D. What Are The Implications Of Different Interpretations?

E. Are There Passages In I Corinthians 7 And Elsewhere That Give Insight Into The Meaning Of "Bondage" And If It Refers To The Marriage Bond Or Not?

Lesson Seven

Meaning Of Phrases: "Not Under Bondage," And "Abide In The Calling"

I. The Text: I Cor. 7:12-24

II. The Problem:
   A. What Does "Not Under Bondage" Mean In I Cor. 7:15?

   B. What Does The Phrase "Abide In The Calling Wherein You Were Called" Mean?

III. What Are Possible Interpretations And The Implications Of Those Differing Interpretations?
   A. I Cor. 7:15 "Not Under Bondage"
      1. One interpretation is that "not under bondage" refers to the "marriage bond."
         a. If this is a correct interpretation, the teacher will advise a faithful Christian mate whose faithful sinner mate is about to leave or has left that the Christian brother/sister is not bound by God's laws

about marriage, and will be or is free to marry again.

b. If this is an incorrect interpretation, the teacher is advising a person that he has a right to remarry when he does not and is advocating that living in an adulterous relationship is acceptable to God.

2. Another interpretation is that "not under bondage" refers to the Christian being bound to or enslaved to the whims, wishes, or desires of the sinner mate.

a. If this is a correct interpretation, the teacher will advise that brother/sister that they are NOT free to marry.

1. Their marriage is accepted by God and is governed by God's marriage laws.

2. The teacher will encourage the Christian to remain unmarried or be reconciled to his mate.

3. If a sinner mate has divorced a Christian and neither committed adultery, and subsequently the Christian marries another person, the teacher will caution him that he is living in adultery and must leave it this unacceptable "marriage" in order to be right with God.

b. If this is an incorrect interpretation, the teacher is advising a person to leave his or her legitimate marriage. How tragic that would be!

B. I Cor. 7:20,24 "Abide In The Calling Wherein You Were Called."

    1. One interpretation might be that "abide in the calling wherein you were called" advises one to remain in ANY relationship in which he is at the time he seeks to become a Christian: adulterous, homosexual, lesbian, etc.

        a. If this is a correct interpretation, the teacher will advise a person to remain in any relationship to which he has been committed.

        b. If this is a correct interpretation, the teacher will advise the person that living in adulterous, homosexual, or lesbian relationships is acceptable in God's sight.

    2. Another interpretation is that "abide in the calling wherein you were called" advises anyone who seeks to become a Christian that all the past, including past marriages, is ignored by God.

        a. If this is a correct interpretation, the teacher will advise them that they can remain in whatever marital relationship they are in at the time they seek to become Christians.

            1. This teacher will reject relationships such as homosexual or lesbian relationships.

            2. He will advise a man and woman to just be sure that they will remain committed to and stay with the mate they NOW have.

            3. The teacher will give them that advice no matter how many

marriages and divorces have occurred previously.
4. The teacher will advise them that God does not hold people responsible for the past.
b. If this is an incorrect interpretation, the teacher is advising a person that living in an adulterous relationship is acceptable.

3. Another interpretation is that "abide in the calling wherein you were called" is discussing wholesome relationships; it is NOT referring to sinful relationships.
a. If this is a correct interpretation, the teacher will advise them that they cannot be in a sinful relationship and be right with God.
b. If this is an incorrect interpretation, the teacher will advise people to leave a legitimate marriage. How tragic that would be!

C. Why Is This Such A SERIOUS Problem?
1. Teachers teaching error will be held accountable for their teaching. Js. 3:1

2. There are diametrically opposed interpretations that are given about these passages.

3. The result of one's interpretation has serious implications!

- a. Brethren are teaching contradictory concepts.
    1. That should not be occurring!
    2. There are internal congregational struggles and intra-congregational struggles because of contradictory teaching by brethren.
- b. If a teacher advises students that sinful relationships are acceptable to God when they are in reality unacceptable:
    1. He is advocating sin.
    2. He is giving sinners false hope. Some will live and die thinking they are in a right relationship with God when they are truly lost.
- c. If a teacher advises students that they should leave wholesome relationships or that they are not free to marry when they are:
    1. He is advocating sin.
    2. He is binding rules upon men that God did not bind!

4. Can both interpretations be right?
    a. It is IMPOSSIBLE!
    b. ONE may be wrong or BOTH may be wrong; BOTH CANNOT BE RIGHT!

D. How Can We Ascertain Or KNOW What Is The Correct Interpretation?

IV. What Tools From Our Toolbox Will Be Helpful In Solving This Problem?

A. The **Immediate Context**.

B. **Greek Words**.

C. The **Biblical Context**.

D. **Other Translations**.

V. Using Our Tools Evaluate The Possible Solutions And To Solve This Problem:

A. **The Context Of I Cor. 7:12-24**

1. Paul has addressed numerous problems in the Church in Corinth. Chapters 1-6.

2. The Corinthians have asked several questions about marriage and sexuality. Platonic Dualism and immorality were rampant in Corinth. These two concepts were underlying many of the problems in the Church in Corinth. Paul addresses them in I Cor. 7.

   a. Are Christianity and sexuality compatible? 1-7

      1. The root of this question was their Platonic dualism; the idea that the spirit is pure; the body is evil.

      2. So, they asked, "Should Christians marry?"

b. What should widowers and widows do with their desires? 8,9

c. Should married people separate or divorce? 10,11

d. What if my mate is NOT a Christian? 12-16

e. Does becoming a Christian demand that one change ALL social relationships? 17-24

f. What about those who have never been married before? 25-38

g. What is God's will about widows marrying? 39,40

B. **Words Of The Immediate Context:**
1. **I Cor. 7:12-16**
   a. **"To the rest"**
      1. Those he had not previously addressed.
      2. Christians married to non-Christians.
   b. **"I speak, not the Lord."**
      1. Is Paul just giving his opinion?
      2. ABSOLUTELY NOT! See I Cor. 2:10,12,13,16
      3. Christ had not addressed this question while on earth.
   c. **The text discusses the marriage of a Christian to a non-Christian.** The Christian should be determined to protect, preserve, and perpetuate the marriage with a non-Christian.
      1. That is true for the Christian man married to a non-Christian wife. 12

2. It is equally true for the Christian woman married to a non-Christian husband. 13
3. The Christian should always seek the continuance of the marriage; however, the non-Christian might seek to dissolve that marriage because of the mate's Christian faith, life, worship, and participation with the Church.

d. **They ARE married in God's sight!** It IS a legitimate marriage! 14
   1. **"Sanctified"**
       a. Perfect, passive verb.
       b. "Was sanctified and still is"
       c. This is NOT referring to moral holiness; moral growth is attained by personal choice and maturity.
       d. It is not referring to "sanctifying the relationship"; if so, that would likely be in the present tense. Hopefully it will continue until the non-Christian sees his/her need for Christ.
       e. The have been married and still are in God's sight.
   2. If their marriage was not legitimate, their children would be "unclean" (illegitimate).

e. **If the non-Christian departs, the Christian is "not under bondage."** 15
   1. **"Depart"**
       a. It is a present tense, indicative mood, middle voice verb.

    b.   It means "if he himself chooses to separate" or "if he chooses to separate himself."

2. If the non-Christian makes that choice, "let him separate."

3. "A brother or sister is not under bondage."

    a. **What could "not under bondage" mean?**

      1. **Not tied to the person by marriage.** (This is the idea that they never were married)

         a. How would that fit the context?

         b. What about verse 14?

         c. Wouldn't we have a contradiction?

         d. What about Paul's instructions about marital obligations in 7:2-5?

      2. **No longer tied to the person by marriage.** (This is the idea that they are no longer married).

         a. Some suggest that if the sinner leaves, the Christian is now free to marry again.

         b. They call this the "Pauline privilege."

         c. They claim that the "marriage bond" is severed.

3. **Not enslaved to the desires of the non-Christian**.
b. **"δεδούλωται"** (dedoulootai)
   1. This is a perfect tense, indicative mood, passive voice, singular verb.
   2. The perfect tense suggests "was not in the past and still is not."
   3. This word would be translated, "has not been in the past and still is not enslaved to" the unbelieving one.
   4. If this refers to the marriage bond, what is it saying?
      a. They never have been and still are not married.
      b. What about verse 14?
      c. Wouldn't we have a contradiction?
   5. What is the root of this word? Is this the word that refers to the marriage bond? Are there verses in this chapter and elsewhere that give insight into this question?
      a. The root of "δεδούλ - ωται" (dedoulootai) is "δούλος" (doulos).
         1. It means "slave."

2. The word would be translated "has not been in the past and still is not enslaved to" the unbelieving one.

3. Other passages where "δεδούλωται"(dedoulootai) is used. II Pet. 2:19 "enslaved to corruption"; Gal. 4:3 "in bondage to the rudiments of the world."

4. The aorist tense is used in Rom. 6:18 and 22 in reference to being "enslaved to sin."

b. **What about the word for "marriage bond?"**

1. It is the Greek word **"δέδεται"** (dedetai).

2. It is a perfect tense, indicative mood, passive voice verb.

3. Its root word is "δέω" (deoo) meaning "bound in marriage." This refers to the marriage bond.

4. It is used in **I Cor. 7:39** and **Rom. 7:2**.
5. A form of the word is also in **I Cor. 7:27**. "δέδεσαι" (dedesai). The only difference is that this is a second person, singular, perfect tense verb; whereas "δέδεται" (dedetai) is a third person, singular, perfect tense verb.
6. "δοῦλος" (doulos) is never used in any other passage to refer to the marriage bond!
7. The passive voice suggests that someone else joined them in marriage. Who did? GOD! Mt. 19:6

c. What does this passage mean?
   1. The Christian is NOT enslaved to the unbeliever; he is already enslaved to Christ!
   2. The Christian is not enslaved to

maintain the marriage under extreme pressure and duress.

3. The Christian is not enslaved to the non-Christian and must give up his/ her faith in order to keep the marriage intact.

f. Two possibilities about verse 16.

1. Why feel guilty for the marriage not continuing?

a. You cannot force your mate to change.

b. You have NO proof that they will convert to Christ.

2. If you remain in the marriage, you may be able to ultimately bring your non-Christian mate to Christ.

g. I Cor. 7:15 gives absolutely NO new "loophole" for a Christian married to a non-Christian!

1. This passage gives NO privilege of remarriage to a Christian whose non-Christian mate leaves.

2. Those who claim that it does simply advocate something that is a "figment of their own desire and imagination!"

2. **I Cor. 7:17-24**

a. Continue to live in the same way (in the same position) that you were when you were called (became a Christian). 17

1. Continue to walk as you have been and continue to be given opportunity in life and in the condition that you were called and continue to live in.

2. NIV "each one should retain the place in life that the Lord assigned to him and to which God has called him."

3. Paul taught the SAME TRUTHS to EACH congregation.

b. **Circumstances in which one may have been "called."**

    1. **Circumcised or uncircumcised.** 18

        a. If circumcised, he must not become distraught about becoming uncircumcised. (Some Jews were having surgery that made them appear to be uncircumcised).

        b. If one is uncircumcised, he need not contemplate or become circumcised.

        c. Salvation in Christ is available for BOTH Jews and Gentiles; it is not determined by one's being circumcised or uncircumcised. It is determined by obedience to Christ! 19. Gal. 6:14,15; Rom. 2:29

        d. Continue in whatever circumstance you were (circumcised or uncircumcised) when you heard the Gospel and became a Christian. 20

2. A **Slave or freeman**. 21
   a. What is Paul saying?
      1. One should not worry if he was a slave when he was called. Slaves can be faithful and pleasing to Christ.
      2. What does the phrase "but if thou mayest be made free, use it rather."
         a. This seems to suggest, "If you have an opportunity to improve your status by becoming a freeman, DO IT!"
         b. Other translations have a different idea:
            1. RSV footnote: "Make use of your present condition instead."
            2. NEB footnote "But even if a chance of liberty should come, choose rather to make good use of your servitude."
            3. This suggests, "Be content where you are." Phil. 4:11; I Tim. 6:8; Heb. 13:5
   b. If Paul is suggesting remain in slavery, would he also say to one

in prison that he should remain in prison rather than take freedom if it were offered?

c.   The slave who is called becomes the Lord's freeman; the free man becomes the Lord's slave.

d.   Every Christian must keep in mind that he was bought by a price, the Blood of Christ; therefore Christians should not choose to become slaves of men.

e.   Continue in whatever circumstance you were (a slave or a freeman) when you heard the Gospel and became a Christian. 24

3.   Tie in also Verse 27. **Married or Single**.

a.   Have you been bound to a wife? Do not seek to be loosed from her. If you are have been loosed and still are from a wife, do not seek a wife.

b.   If one's mate has died or committed adultery, he should not seek to marry. But WHY is this advice given by Paul? It is because of the "present distress." 26

c.   What does "abide in the calling wherein you were called" mean?

1.   Some would advocate abiding in whatever situation you are when you desire to become a Christian.

      a.   Single.
      b.   Married.
      c.   Married and divorced.
      d.   Married, divorced, and remarried (and how many times does not really matter).
      e.   In a polygamous or polyandrous relationship.
      f.   In a homosexual, or lesbian relationship.

            1.   Such advocates do not see any of the above situations as sinful.

            2.   But God does! Gen. 19:1-25; Lev. 18:22,23; 20:13,15,16; Rom. 1:22-27; I Cor. 6:9,10; I Tim. 1:10; Jude 7.

2.   One interpretation suggests that it does not matter what your marital circumstance was before you became a Christian, you can remain in your present relationship and be a faithful Christian.

      a.   Single.
      b.   Married.
      c.   Married and divorced.
      d.   Married, divorced, and remarried (and how many times does not really matter).
      e.   Those who hold this view believe that baptism will wash away the past indiscretions and broken marriages.

3.   However, observe the types of callings Paul is discussing:

a. **HONORABLE relationships!**
 1. National status: circum-cised, uncircumcised.
 2. Social status: slave, freeman.
 3. Marital status: married, single.
b. This text in NO WAY suggests that one can remain in sinful relationships as a Christian!
 1. To try to compare adulterous relationships with the above honorable relationships is like comparing apples and oranges!
 2. It is a TOTAL misuse of this text to attempt to justify sin!
 3. If one can condone adulterous relationships, why not polygamous, homosexual, or lesbian relationships? People continuing to be drug dealers or hit men for the mob?

C. **The Biblical Context**:
 1. Marriage is to be a LIFETIME commitment.
  a. Rom. 7:2,3
  b. God HATES divorce! Mal. 2:16

 2. God's laws for marriage are for "Whosoever marries" whether Christian or non-Christian. Mt. 5:32; Mt. 19:9

a. "Whosoever" is always governed by the context.

b. "Whosoever" in Mt. 10:32 is "anyone who confesses that Jesus is the Christ."

c. "Whosoever" in Mt. 10:33 is "anyone who denies that Jesus is the Christ."

d. "Whosoever" in Matthew chapters 5 and 19 is "anyone who has a wife" (Christian OR non-Christian).

3. The general principal is that anyone who leaves his mate and marries another has entered into an adulterous relationship. Mt. 5:32; 19:9; Rom. 7:2,3

4. The **only exception** is when one's mate has committed fornication while the person has been faithful and innocent himself/herself. Mt. 19:9

5. If a husband and a wife separate, there are only two legitimate choices: remain unmarried or be reconciled to your mate. I Cor. 7:10,11

   a. God gives NO provision for entering into a new "marriage."

   b. The ONLY ones who have a right to remarry are:

      1. Those whose mate has died.

      2. An innocent mate who puts away his/her mate for fornication while they were living together as husband and wife.

6. Truths about adultery, sin, and baptism.

   a. What IS "adultery?"

1. It is "unlawful sexual intercourse."
2. The Greek word "μοιχεία" (moicheia) is defined as "adultery" or "having unlawful intercourse."
3. Jesus affirmed that an "unlawful marriage" is "adultery." He stated that:
    a. An innocent but "put away" mate who marries someone other than his/her mate has entered an "unlawful marriage." They are living in adultery.
    b. One who has been previously married and has left his/her innocent mate (the mate did not commit fornication while they were living together as husband and wife) and then takes another mate has entered an "unlawful marriage." They are living in "adultery." Mt. 5:32; 19:9
4. Adultery is NOT just "covenant breaking." If one defines "adultery" as covenant breaking:
    a. Why does a husband "cause" his innocent but "put away" wife to be "guilty of adultery?" Mt. 5:32
        1. Some affirm that she is simply no longer able to fulfill her duties as a wife to him.
        2. They claim that she is forced to break the covenant to be his companion, supporter,

and sexual companion because of his sinful decision.

3. The affirmation is that because of his sinful decision, she is forced to sin also.

4. However, no one can be FORCED to sin by another person!

b. Why is the one who marries the "having been put away" person guilty of "adultery?" Mt. 19:9. If he was never married in the past, what covenant did he break?

c. Why does the Greek language use the present tense?

1. "Causeth" is the Greek word "ποιεῖ" (poiei), a present tense Greek verb. He "makes" her commit adultery.

2. "Doth commit adultery" in Mt. 19:9 is the Greek present tense verb "μοιχᾶται" (moichatai).

5. Adultery can be a one time act; one can also continue in it.

a. A person could have a single unlawful sexual encounter with someone other than their mate. That is "adultery."

b. A person can continue in adultery.

1. He or she may continue that unlawful sexual conduct.
2. One can "live in" adultery. Col. 3:7
3. A child of God can continue to be a spiritual adulterer.

6. What was adultery BEFORE baptism is adultery AFTER baptism!
   a. Baptism makes NO WRONG RELATIONSHIP RIGHT!
   b. Baptism must ALWAYS be preceded by repentance.
      1. Repentance demands a sorrowful heart that determines to no longer live in sin.
      2. Repentance demands leaving the practice of sin.

b. The word "married" does not affirm the holiness or sinfulness of a relationship.
   1. Many argue, "Well, Jesus SAID they were 'married' in Mt. 5:32 and 19:9.
   2. Certainly Jesus used the words "shall marry" and "shall marry another" in Mt. 3:32 and 19:9.
      a. The Greek word "γαμήση" (gamaysay) is used in Mt. 5:32 and the Greek phrase "γαμήση ἄλλην" (gamaysay allayn) is used in Mt. 19:9.
      b. The word "γαμήση" (gamaysay) is an aorist subjunctive verb meaning "if he marries."

3. Does the use of the word "marry" affirm that the relationship is holy or accepted by God?

   a. In Mk. 6:17,18 and Lk. 3:19 John told Herod that Herodias was "the wife of Philip his brother."

   b. And yet, Herod "had married her."

   c. John told Herod, "It is **not lawful** for thee to have they brother's wife."

   d. Observations:

      1. "Marriage" here is used in "accommodative language" explaining the decision Herod and Herodias had made.

      2. Yes, they "married;" this does not explain if it was a "lawful marriage" or an "unlawful marriage."

      3. "Married" is "accommodative language" explaining decisions they have made and actions they have taken and society's view of this new "relationship?"

c. What if one has "put away" his/her mate and no fornication occurred?

   1. The Lord's disciples grasped Jesus teaching in Mt. 19:1-9

   2. Their response was, "If the case of the man be so with *his* wife, it is not good to marry." 19:10

        a.   They reasoned: "Why should one marry? If the marriage fails and no adultery is involved, you are doomed to a life of celibacy."

        b.   They understood His teaching: To remarry, you would be "in adultery."

    3.   Jesus then explained that in such a case, one would have to live without sexual intercourse. He has no right to remarry. 19:12

VI. Conclusion:

A. The Topic Of Divorce And Remarriage Is A Heart-rending Topic.

B. We Must Give An Account For The Advice That We Give Those We Counsel.

C. We Need To Have Loving Kindness And Compassion Coupled With A Deep Devotion To The Truth!

D. The Seriousness Of Our Interpretation Of These Texts.

    1.   We must desire and determine to know and teach Truth!

    2.   The Bible is consistent; It does not contradict Itself!

3. Brethren are teaching contradictory concepts.
   a. That should not be occurring!
   b. There are internal congregational struggles and intra-congregational struggles because of contradictory teaching by brethren.

4. People's SOULS and ETERNAL DESTINIES are determined by what they teach, believe, and obey.
   a. Perversion of Truth leads to one teaching false doctrine. We will be held accountable by the Lord for what we teach!
   b. It suggests that people can remain in sin and be in the Church.
   c. It fills the Church with adulterers.
   d. It offers hope to people when God gives no such hope.
   e. It keeps people separated from God and ends in their eternal separation from God in Hell.

E. Some Cautions:
   1. Be sure to get the facts!
      a. Question: if two people have been married and divorced, and they were not divorced for the reason of fornication, and later they remarried, in what condition are they spiritually?
         1. Invariably most will quickly answer "Adultery!"
         2. That is not true in every situation.

3. What if two people were married to each other, divorced without any unfaithfulness having occurred, and then they remarry each other? Are they in sin? NO!

b. The point: make sure you get the facts before you answer questions about marriage, divorce, and remarriage.

2. Realize that people tend to rationalize to attempt to make their situation fit God's Word so they can feel right in whatever marriage situation they are presently!

Assignment:

A. Controversial Events: Judges 11:29-40

B. What Is The Problem? Why Is This A Controversial Passage?

C. What Are The Possible Conclusions?

D. What Arguments Are Used To Support The Differing Interpretations?

E. Which Position Do YOU Hold And Why?

Lesson Eight

Controversial Events: Jephthah

(Note: I begin this class by asking every student to take the position; Jephthah DID kill his daughter, or he DID NOT kill her.)

I. **The Text: Judges 11:29-40**

 A. This Involves The Vow That The Judge, Jephthah, Made.

 B. Good Brethren Honestly Disagree About The Consequences Of His Vow.

 C. One's Interpretation Of This Passage Is Not A Matter Of Salvation.   This Is NOT A Salvation Issue.

 D. A Caution: Be Careful Not To Attack Brethren Who Hold A Differing View About Jephthah As Rejecting The Bible Or As Attempting To Twist Or Distort Scripture.

II. **The Problem!**

 A. What Are The Implications Of Jephthah's Vow?

B. Did It Mean That He Sacrificed Her To God? Or Did She Simply Have To Remain A Virgin The Rest Of Her Life?

    1. His vow was, "Then it shall be, that **whatsoever cometh forth of the doors of my house to meet me**, when I return in peace from the children of Ammon, **shall surely be the LORD'S**, and **I will offer it up for a burnt offering**." 31

    2. Upon his return home, his daughter was the first to come out the door. Jephthah said, "I have opened my mouth unto the LORD, and I cannot go back." 35

    3. His daughter urged him, "My father, *if* thou hast opened thy mouth unto the LORD, do to me according to that which hath proceeded out of thy mouth;" 36

    4. "She returned unto her father, who did with her *according* to his vow which he had vowed:" 39

    5. So, did he fulfill his vow or not?

III. Possible Solutions To The Problem.
A. He DID Kill Her!

B. He Did NOT Kill Her!

IV. **What Tools Can We Use To Seek A Solution To This Problem?**
   A. The **Immediate Context**: The Events Of This Chapter.

   B. The **Surrounding Context**: Study The Surrounding Chapters To Learn More About Jephthah.

   C. The **Expanded Biblical Context**.
      1. What it teaches about sacrifices.

      2. What it teaches about human sacrifice.

      3. What is said by God about Jephthah.

V. **Using Tools To Solve The Problem. What Position Do You Take? Why? Give Reasons To Defend Your Position!**
   A. **Why Would One Assume He Sacrificed Her?**
      1. **A "literal" interpretation** of the text.
         a. Because that was his vow!
         b. God required that one keep his vow! Dt. 23:21-23 "When thou shalt vow a vow unto the LORD thy God, thou shalt not slack to pay it: for the LORD thy God will surely require it of thee; and it would be sin in thee. ²²But if thou shalt forbear to vow, it shall be no sin in thee. ²³That which is gone out of thy lips thou shalt keep and perform; *even* a freewill offering,

        according as thou hast vowed unto the LORD thy God, which thou hast promised with thy mouth."

c. Thus, for two months, she bemoaned the fact that she had lived and would die a virgin.

d. Then he sacrificed her. He kept his vow!

e. Doesn't the text say, "he returned unto her father, who did with her *according* to his vow which he had vowed:" 39

f. Questions about this position:
   1. Does it SAY that he killed her?
   2. It says that he kept his vow; not that he killed her.

2. He was a **godly man**; he surely would have kept his word!
   a. He promised, he had to keep his promise.
   b. His daughter encouraged him that he must keep his word.
   c. Questions about this position:
      1. All that is true.
      2. However, does it necessitate that he killed her?

3. It is a view **held by the oldest interpreters**.
   a. This is an important consideration in studying Scripture.
   b. Josephus said that he killed her. *Antiquities of the Jews*, Book v, Chapter vii, Verses 9,10.
   c. Questions about this position:
      1. Always remember that commentators are NOT inspired!

2. Too, older commentators have been wrong about some views.
3. Examples:
   a. Song of Solomon was allegorized as emphasizing the relationship between Christ and the Church. It was describing the love between a husband and wife.
   b. Amos 6:5 was purported to condemn David's use of instrumental music in worship in the O.T. However, that interpretation is a direct contradiction of Ps. 150, II Chr. 7:6, and II Chr. 29:25,27.
   c. Revelation was described as directly pointing to and condemning the Roman Catholic Church. While some principles may apply, the book was written to persecuted Christians to tell them that the Roman Empire would be punished.

4. There was **pagan influence all around; he must have adopted their practices**.
   a. They were living in Canaan with all its idolatry and pagan influence.
   b. Sometimes prophets were tempted by it; example, Samson.
   c. One should not be amazed that a judge would sin; Gideon did when he used his ephod to sanction idolatry. Ju. 8:27

      d.   Questions about this position:
1. Did God tolerate Samson's sin?
2. Or did He punish Samson because of his sin? Samson did later repent and God used him to judge the Philistines.
3. Did Gideon really make this decorated ephod to sanction idolatry or for personal praise? Was this more of a memorial that the people began to worship?
4. If Jephthah sinned, why didn't God punish him? Samson suffered because of his sins!
5. If he had adopted pagan ways, would God have continued to use him as a judge?

5. **Why assume that Jephthah had in mind an animal? God would not have accepted the sacrifice of a dog, donkey, or other unclean animal.**
   a. This is in response to those who say he expected first to see an animal come forth from the house upon his arrival home.
   b. And obviously, God would not accept such a sacrifice!
   c. Those who hold this view affirm that Jephthah surely knew a person would be the first to come forth to greet him.
   d. Questions about this position:
      1 Nothing suggests that Jephthah was thinking only of an animal.

2   It is absolutely true that God would not accept the sacrifice of an unclean animal.

3   But, did God provide a way for redemption of a vow that was made for a person? Yes!

6. The **severity of his agony** when he saw his daughter exit the house.

   a.   If he had only believed that he had to pay money to redeem her, he would not have reacted with such strong emotion. He rent his clothes; he declared that she "brought me very low."

   b.   There is no way to understand such agonizing grief except that he knew he had to kill his daughter.

   c.   Questions about this position:

      1.   These are valid points.

      2.   However, would he not have had the same reactions when he realized that keeping his vow would devote his daughter to a life of virginity and childlessness.

      3.   Therefore, he would never have grandchildren; his family lineage would cease to exist.

7. **His daughter's encouragement**.

   a.   Ju. 11:36 "And she said unto him, My father, *if* thou hast opened thy mouth unto the LORD, do to me according to that which hath proceeded out of thy mouth; forasmuch as the LORD hath

taken vengeance for thee of thine enemies, *even* of the children of Ammon."
b. 11:37 "And she said unto her father, Let this thing be done for me: let me alone two months, that I may go up and down upon the mountains, and bewail my virginity, I and my fellows."
c. Questions about this position:
1. She did encourage him to keep his vow.
2. But, does it state that she told him to go ahead and kill her.
3. Observe, "let me alone two months, that I may go up and down upon the mountains, and **bewail my virginity**, I and my fellows." 37
4. The result of the vow was that "she knew no man." 39

8. The **agony of his daughter**.
a. She would not have had such severe agony if she were going to be allowed to live. She "bewailed her virginity."
b. Questions about this position:
1. Are you so sure?
2. What about the agony of women of the Bible who were barren?
a. Sarai. Gen. 16:1-6
b. Hannah. I Sa. 1:6-16
c. Rachel.
1. Gen. 30:1 "Give me children, or else I die."
2. She was so desperate to have a child that she offered Jacob her handmaid, Bilhah

so she could have children. 3,4

    3.   22,23 "God hath taken away my reproach:"

  d. Elisabeth. Lk. 1:25 "he looked on *me*, to take away my reproach among men."

9. There is **no Biblical record of any virgins being devoted to the service of God.**
   a. This is affirmed by many.
   b. Questions about this position:
      1. Is this really a valid point?
      2. Are there examples of devoted women? Yes!

10. **Lev. 27:29** "None devoted, which shall be devoted of men, shall be redeemed; *but* shall surely be put to death."
    a. This passage affirms that a person may not be redeemed; he is to be killed.
    b. Questions about this position:
       1. What about passages that say humans ARE to be redeemed?
       2. What is Lev. 27:29 really talking about?

11. He sinned! But **why be amazed that a judge sinned?**
    a. Eli did, I Sa. 2:12; 3:11-14; Samuel did, I Sa. 8:1-5; Gideon did, 8:27; Samson did, Ju. 14-16.
    b. Questions about this position:
       1. Did Gideon REALLY sin?

- a. He made an ephod as a memorial to his victory over the Midianites. 8:26,27
- b. The Israelites began to worship it. 8:27
- c. The Bible does not condemn Gideon; he did not sin; he simply made a memento; the Israelites later began to worship it.
- d. They sinned, not Gideon.
  2. Did God just ignore Samson's sins?
    - a. NO!
    - b. This lustful and arrogant man was punished for his sins; he ended up in the heathen temple blind and grinding grain like an ox. 16:21
    - c. The Philistines gloried in their gods; they praised their gods for giving them victory over Samson and his God! 16:23,24
    - d. They ridiculed him terribly. 16:24
    - e. Samson repented, called upon God, and was given his strength again; he killed more Philistines in his death than he had in his life. 16:25-30
- c. The difference is that when Samson sinned, God told us that he sinned. The Bible does not tell us that Jephthah sinned.

B. **Why Would One Assume That He Did NOT Sacrifice Her?**
   1. **Assumptions** are made that may not be correct:
      a. **He assumed that an animal would be the first thing to exit his house**.
         1. Verse 31 may give that impression: "Then it shall be, that whatsoever cometh forth of the doors of my house to meet me, when I return in peace from the children of Ammon, shall surely be the LORD'S, **and** I will offer it up for a burnt offering."
         2. The word "and" could be translated "or". If so it would read, "Then it shall be, that whatsoever cometh forth of the doors of my house to meet me, when I return in peace from the children of Ammon, shall surely be the LORD'S, **OR** I will offer it up for a burnt offering." This is from "Young's Literal Translation."
         3. Thus, he may have been completely aware that it could be a person or an animal.
         4. Questions about this position:
            a. None of the major translations use this distinction.
            b. How could he plan to "offer it up" if it had been an unclean animal or a female animal?
            c. Did he not know that a person could be redeemed?

b. **He was a rash man making a rash vow**.
   1. He was foolish; he was so eager for a victory that he made a ridiculous vow that he should ever have made.
   2. Questions about this position:
      a. Is Jephthah REALLY a rash man? He is not described as a rash man!
      b. Was he rash in life? Read about his life. Judges 11:1-12:7
         1. He was a mighty warrior. 1
         2. His mother was a prostitute. 1
         3. His half brothers ridiculed him about being the son of a harlot; they declared that he would not be an inheritor of his father's estate. They ran him out of their home. 2,3
         4. He became the judge of Israel. 11:4-11
            a. When the Ammonites attacked, the Gileadites sought Jephthah to be their captain and to deliver them. 5-6
            b. Jephthah asked, "Did not you hate me and expel me from my father's house? Why are you calling me now that you are in trouble?" 7

  c. He agreed to return if after the victory they would make him their head. 8-11

 5. His sent a delegation to the Ammonites. 12-28

  a. The question was asked, "WHY are you attacking us?" 12

  b. The delegation returned with the message that the king of the Ammonites was angry because Israel captured the land east of Jordan and 2 tribes dwelt there. He wanted the lands restored to him. 13

  c. Jephthah sent a response:

   1. When Israel left Egypt, they requested passage through the countries of the Edomites, Moabites, and the Amorites. 14-20

   2. GOD gave the Israelites the land of the Amorites; why then should they give this land

to the Ammonites? 21-23

3. If you thought Chemosh, your god, gave you a land, would you relinquish it? No! And we will not relinquish land that God has given us! 24

4. The present Moabite king, Balak, made no attempt to reclaim the land that Israel took from Sihon when Israel was marching from Egypt to Canaan! 25,26

5. We have not wronged you; you have wronged us by going to war against us. 27

6. Let God be the judge as to who the aggressor is and who is wrong in this event! 27

d. The king of the Ammonites rejected the message from Jephthah. 28

6. Jephthah's Vow And Victory! 29-40
   a. The spirit of the Lord came upon him; he led Israel into battle! 29
   b. He made a vow that if God would deliver Ammon into his hands, whatever would come forth out of his house to meet him when he returned in peace from the victory would be the Lord's and he would offer a burnt offering. 30,31
   c. He won a decisive victory. 32,33
   d. Upon his return home, his daughter, his only child, came out of the house in joyous celebration! "Dad is home and has been victorious!" 34
   e. Jephthah's response: 35
      1. His joy quickly turned to anguish; he rent his clothes!
      2. It broke his heart to see his daughter, yet, he could no go back upon his vow.
   f. The daughter's re-action: 36,37

1. She urged him to keep his vow; "Remember God has given us the victory."
2. She asked for two months to take her friends and wander the mountains "bewailing her virginity."

g. She bewailed her virginity for two months. 38

h. Then she returned to her father; he kept his vow. She knew no man. 39

i. A four-day lamentation was held yearly to weep for her. 40

7. The Ephraimites quarreled with Jephthah because he did not ask for their help in the fight. 12:1-7

a. They threatened to burn his house. 1

b. He reminded them that when the Ammonites attacked, he asked for the Ephraimites to help, they refused. 2,3

c. Jephthah gathered the Gileadites; they defeated the Ephraimites. 4

- d. The Gileadites captured all the passes over Jordan. 5-7
    1. When people came to the passes, they were asked to say "Shibboleth."
    2. The Ephraimites could not say it; they said Sib-boleth."
    3. 42,000 Ephraimites were slain.
  8. Jephthah died after being the judge of Israel for 6 years. 12:7. Ibzan was the next judge.
3. Summations:
    a. He did not rashly accept the request to come home and protect the Gileadites against the Ammonites.
    b. He did not just summarily attack the Ammonites. He tried negotiation and reason.
    c. He did not utter his vow in the midst of great confusion in battle.
        1. He made it while still at home.
        2. This was just after the spirit of the Lord came upon him. 29-31

4. Questions about this position:
    a. How do you know that he was not rash in this one vow?
    b. He should have contemplated the consequences before making that vow.

2. His **God**, the living God, **hated human sacrifice!**
    a. Dt. 12:31 "Thou shalt not do so unto the LORD thy God: for every abomination to the LORD, which he hateth, have they done unto their gods; for even their sons and their daughters they have burnt in the fire to their gods."
    b. Such was abomination in God's sight! "Moreover thou hast taken thy sons and thy daughters, whom thou hast borne unto me, and these hast thou sacrificed unto them to be devoured. *Is this* of thy whoredoms a small matter, [21]That thou hast slain my children, and delivered them to cause them to pass through *the fire* for them?" Ezek. 16:20,21
    c. Lev. 18:21 "And thou shalt not let any of thy seed pass through *the fire* to Molech, neither shalt thou profane the name of thy God: I *am* the LORD."
    d. Lev. 20:2-5 "Again, thou shalt say to the children of Israel, Whosoever *he be* of the children of Israel, or of the strangers that sojourn in Israel, that giveth *any* of his seed unto Molech; he shall surely be put to death: the people of the land shall stone him with stones. [3]And I will set my

face against that man, and will cut him off from among his people; because he hath given of his seed unto Molech, to defile my sanctuary, and to profane my holy name. [4]And if the people of the land do any ways hide their eyes from the man, when he giveth of his seed unto Molech, and kill him not: [5]Then I will set my face against that man, and against his family, and will cut him off, and all that go a whoring after him, to commit whoredom with Molech, from among their people."

e.   Dt. 18:9-14 "When thou art come into the land which the LORD thy God giveth thee, thou shalt not learn to do after the abominations of those nations. [10]There shall not be found among you *any one* that maketh his son or his daughter to pass through the fire, *or* that useth divination, *or* an observer of times, or an enchanter, or a witch, [11]Or a charmer, or a consulter with familiar spirits, or a wizard, or a necromancer. [12]For all that do these things *are* an abomination unto the LORD: and because of these abominations the LORD thy God doth drive them out from before thee. [13]Thou shalt be perfect with the LORD thy God. [14]For these nations, which thou shalt possess, hearkened unto observers of times, and unto diviners: but as for thee, the LORD thy God hath not suffered thee so *to do*."

f.   Observe God's feelings about Kings of Judah offering the children of Judah as human sacrifices:

1.   Ahaz

   a.   II Ki. 16:3   "But he walked in the way of the kings of Israel, yea, and made his son to pass through the fire, according to the abominations of the heathen, whom the LORD cast out from before the children of Israel."

   b.   II Chr. 28:3-5   "Moreover he burnt incense in the valley of the son of Hinnom, and burnt his children in the fire, after the abominations of the heathen whom the LORD had cast out before the children of Israel. ⁴He sacrificed also and burnt incense in the high places, and on the hills, and under every green tree. ⁵Wherefore the LORD his God delivered him into the hand of the king of Syria; and they smote him, and carried away a great multitude of them captives, and brought *them* to Damascus. And he was also delivered into the hand of the king of Israel, who smote him with a great slaughter."

2.   Manasseh

   a.   II Ki. 21:6   "And he made his son pass through the fire, and observed times, and used enchantments, and dealt with familiar spirits and wizards: he wrought much wickedness in the sight of the LORD, to provoke *him* to anger."

b. II Chr. 33:6 "And he caused his children to pass through the fire in the valley of the son of Hinnom: also he observed times, and used enchantments, and used witchcraft, and dealt with a familiar spirit, and with wizards: he wrought much evil in the sight of the LORD, to provoke him to anger."

c. II Ki. 21:9 "But they hearkened not: and Manasseh seduced them to do more evil than did the nations whom the LORD destroyed before the children of Israel."

d. II Ki. 21:14,15 "And I will forsake the remnant of mine inheritance, and deliver them into the hand of their enemies; and they shall become a prey and a spoil to all their enemies; [15]Because they have done *that which was* evil in my sight, and have provoked me to anger, since the day their fathers came forth out of Egypt, even unto this day."

g. How then would God accept such ungodly action from his chosen man, a judge?

       h. How would God have allowed him to be a judge for 6 years, 12:7, after he "kept his vow" if he had offered her as a human sacrifice?

       i. Questions about this position:
          1. Did not God demand that one keep a vow?
          2. He is just doing what he promised.

3. **No LOYAL judge of God would have thought of making such a sacrifice!**

       a. He would have known how God felt about human sacrifice.

       b. Would a godly man like Jephthah EVEN THINK of human sacrifice?
          1. He gave God the glory for Israel's victories. Ju. 11:12-28
          2. He wanted God to be his judge. Ju. 11:27
          3. The spirit of the Lord was upon him. Ju. 11:29
          4. The Lord gave him the victory! Ju. 11:32
          5. He kept his vow! Ju. 11:39
          6. He is the "Hall of Faith!" Heb. 11:32

       c. Would God give victory to one who would practice human sacrifice?

       d. Does the Bible explicitly say that he actually sacrificed her as a human sacrifice?

       e. How could he sacrifice a female? All burnt offerings had to be MALE!

       f. Who could have made the offering? No Levite would have done it!

g. Where would she have been offered? On a heathen altar?

h. Questions about this position:

1. Does not this position assume that a judge was above sin?

2. What about Samson? He is also in the "Hall of Faith!"

4. **God made provisions for fulfilling a vow of a person.**

a. The Israelites were not allowed to kill any person to fulfil a vow.

b. "And the LORD spake unto Moses, saying, ²Speak unto the children of Israel, and say unto them, When a man shall make a singular vow, the persons *shall be* for the LORD by thy estimation. ³And thy estimation shall be of the male from twenty years old even unto sixty years old, even thy estimation shall be fifty shekels of silver, after the shekel of the sanctuary. ⁴And if it *be* a female, then thy estimation shall be thirty shekels. ⁵And if *it be* from five years old even unto twenty years old, then thy estimation shall be of the male twenty shekels, and for the female ten shekels. ⁶And if *it be* from a month old even unto five years old, then thy estimation shall be of the male five shekels of silver, and for the female thy estimation *shall be* three shekels of silver. ⁷And if *it be* from sixty years old and above; if *it be* a male, then thy estimation shall be fifteen shekels, and for the female ten shekels." Lev. 27:1-7

5. **Lev. 27:29**, mentioned above to support Jephthah killing his daughter, **is not talking about fulfilling a vow**.

    a. It is talking about redemption of one convicted of a heinous crime.

    b. Such a vile person could not be redeemed; he was to be killed.

    c. Other translations assist in understanding this passage.

        1. "No person under the ban, who may become doomed to destruction among men, shall be redeemed, *but* shall surely be put to death." NKJV

        2. "No person devoted to destruction may be ransomed; he must be put to death." NIV

6. **She did not bewail her death; she bewailed her virginity!**

    a. Ju. 11:37 "And she said unto her father, Let this thing be done for me: let me alone two months, that I may go up and down upon the mountains, and **bewail my virginity**, I and my fellows."

    b. She "bewailed her virginity," not her death!

    c. What would be the purpose of this action if she were going to be killed?

    d. She would not have the privilege of marriage.

    e. She would not have children; this was a horrible tragedy to a Jewish woman!

        1. Hannah. I Sa. 1:2-18

        2. Rachel. Gen. 30:1 "And when Rachel saw that she bare Jacob no

children, Rachel envied her sister; and said unto Jacob, Give me children, or else I die."

3. Rebekah. Gen. 25:21
4. Elisabeth. Lk. 1:7
5. Pr. 30:15,16 "There are three *things that* are never satisfied, *yea*, four *things* say not, *It is* enough: [16]The grave; and the barren womb; the earth *that* is not filled with water; and the fire *that* saith not, *It is* enough."

f. This would have been a horrible tragedy for Jephthah; his family lineage would end; he would have no grand-children.

g. A four-day lamentation was held yearly to weep for her because of the vow of virginity. 40

h. She likely was devoted to the service of the Lord at the door of the tabernacle for the rest of her life.

1. Ex. 38:8 "And he made the laver *of* brass, and the foot of it *of* brass, of the lookingglasses of *the women* assembling, which assembled *at* the door of the tabernacle of the congregation."

2. I Sa. 2:22 "Now Eli was very old, and heard all that his sons did unto all Israel; and how they lay with the women that assembled *at* the door of the tabernacle of the congregation."

3. Anna. Lk. 2:36,37 "And there was one Anna, a prophetess, the daughter of Phanuel, of the tribe of Aser: she

was of a great age, and had lived with an husband seven years from her virginity; [37]And she *was* a widow of about fourscore and four years, which departed not from the temple, but served *God* with fastings and prayers night and day."

7. **Why did Jephthah allow his daughter to go and bewail her virginity for two months?**
   a. Why did he not immediately kill her to fulfill his vow?
   b. Why did not he spend time with her before her death?

VI. Lessons We Can Learn From This Story!
A. Be Careful About Making Quick Conclusions About Passages.

B. Be Careful About Accepting Accepted Interpretations Without Thoughtful Study And Consideration!

C. Good Brethren May Disagree About The Final Action; They Need To Be Extremely Respectful Of Each Other!

D. Always Consider The Implications Of A Vow!
   1. Jephthah made a serious vow.

2.   It is often thought that he made a vow without thinking of the implications! As we have seen, that does not appear to be correct.

3.   If you promise God something, you had better do it!

4.   Think about statements like "I'll NEVER forsake my Lord."

E.   The Necessity Of Keeping Vows.
  1.   Ju. 11:35 "I have opened my mouth unto the LORD, and I cannot go back."

  2.   His daughter urged him to keep his vow; she respected the seriousness of vows!

  3.   Dt. 23:21-23 "When thou shalt vow a vow unto the LORD thy God, thou shalt not slack to pay it: for the LORD thy God will surely require it of thee; and it would be sin in thee. [22]But if thou shalt forbear to vow, it shall be no sin in thee. [23]That which is gone out of thy lips thou shalt keep and perform; *even* a freewill offering, according as thou hast vowed unto the LORD thy God, which thou hast promised with thy mouth."

  4.   Nu. 30:2 "If a man vow a vow unto the LORD, or swear an oath to bind his soul with a bond; he shall not break his word, he shall do according to all that proceedeth out of his mouth."

(Note: I end this class by asking every student to take a position: Jephthah DID kill his daughter or he DID NOT kill her. It is interesting to observe how student's minds are changed as a result of this study.)

Assignment:
    A. Texts:
        1. Rom. 8:29-33; 9:11; 11:5,7,28

        2. Eph. 1:3-12

        3. I Pet. 1:2; 2:6

    B. Does The Bible Teach Predestination?

    C. What Are The Problems With The Discussion Of Predestination, Election, And Choice?

    D. How Can These Problems Be Properly Understood And Explained?

Difficult Biblical Concepts: Predestination, Election And Choice

Introduction:

    A. An Introductory Question: "Does The Bible Teach 'Predestination?'"

    B. Many, If Not Most, Christians Will QUICKLY Respond, "NO WAY!"

    C. However, After A Brief Investigation Of Scripture, One Realizes That It Is Impossible To Argue That There Is No Predestination, Election, Or Choice.

I. Texts:

    A. Rom. 8:29-33; 9:11; 11:5,7,28

    B. Eph. 1:3-12

    C. I Pet. 1:2; 2:6

II. The Problem:

A. Does The Bible Really Teach Predestination?

B. Many Believe That "Predestination" Means That Everything About One's Salvation Is Predetermined By God. Some Even Believe That Every Event In A Person's Life Has Been Foreordained.

C. How Can One Correspond Man's Salvation And The Events Of His Life Being Foreordained With The Biblical Teaching Of Personal Choice.

D. What IS The Biblical Teaching Concerning "Predestination?"

III. Possible Solutions To The Problem:

A. God Has Predetermined Who Will Be Saved And When They Will Be Saved; Man Has NO Responsibility At All In Salvation.

B. The Godhead Has Extended Mercy, That Is, They Have Felt Compassion For Us As Sinners; They Provided Grace, That Is, They Acted Upon Their Mercy And Provided A Means Of Salvation For Sinners; Then They Extend That Grace To All Sinners Who Will Willingly Turn To Them In Obedience To Receive Their Grace.

IV. **The Tools To Use To Solve The Problem.**
    A. **Bible Verses** That Teach These Concepts.

    B. **Different Versions** Of The Bible.

    C. **Word Meanings.**

    D. **Context** Of The Passages.

    E. **Consistency With The Rest Of The Scriptures.**

V. **Using Our Tools To Evaluate And To Solve The Problem:**
    A. **Bible Verses That Teach These Concepts.**
        1. **Predestination:**
            a. Eph. 1:5 "Having **predestinated** us unto the adoption of children by Jesus Christ to himself, according to the good pleasure of his will,"
            b. Eph. 1:11 "In whom also we have obtained an inheritance, being **predestinated** according to the purpose of him who worketh all things after the counsel of his own will:"
            c. Rom. 8: 29 "For whom he did **foreknow,** he also did **predestinate** to be conformed to the image of his Son, that he might be the firstborn among many brethren."

d. Rom. 8:30 "Moreover whom he did **predestinate**, them he also called: and whom he called, them he also justified: and whom he justified, them he also glorified."

2. **Election**:
   a. Rom. 11:7 "What then? Israel hath not obtained that which he seeketh for; but the **election** hath obtained it, and the rest were blinded."
   b. I Pet. 1:2 "**Elect** according to the **foreknowledge** of God the Father, through sanctification of the Spirit, unto obedience and sprinkling of the blood of Jesus Christ: Grace unto you, and peace, be multiplied."
   c. I Pet. 2:6 "Wherefore also it is contained in the scripture, Behold, I lay in Sion a chief corner stone, **elect**, precious: and he that believeth on him shall not be confounded."
   d. Rom. 9:11 "(For *the children* being not yet born, neither having done any good or evil, that the purpose of God according to **election** might stand, not of works, but of him that calleth;)"
   e. Rom. 11:28 "As concerning the gospel, *they are* enemies for your sakes: but as touching the **election**, *they are* beloved for the fathers' sakes."

3. **Choice**:
   a. Josh. 24:15 "And if it seem evil unto you to serve the LORD, **choose** you this day

whom ye will serve; whether the gods which your fathers served that *were* on the other side of the flood, or the gods of the Amorites, in whose land ye dwell: but as for me and my house, we will serve the LORD."

b.   John 7:17 "If any man **will** do his will, he shall know of the doctrine, whether it be of God, or *whether* I speak of myself."

c.   Mt. 16:24 "Then said Jesus unto his disciples, If any *man* **will** come after me, let him deny himself, and take up his cross, and follow me."

B.   **Different Versions Of The Bible**.
1.   **Predestinate**.
a.   In Eph. 1:5,11 and Rom. 8:29,30 "predestinated." ASV uses the word "foreordained;" NKJV and NIV use "predestined."
b.   In Rom. 8:29,30 "predestinate." ASV uses the word "foreordained;" NIV uses "predestined."

2.   **Elect**.
a.   Rom.11:7 "election." KJV, NKJV, and ASV. NIV "elect."
b.   I Pet. 1:2 "elect." KJV and NKJV. NIV "have been chosen."
c.   I Pet. 2:6 "elect." KJV, NKJV and ASV. NIV "chosen."
d.   Rom. 9:11, 11:28 "election."

3. **Choice**.
   a. Josh. 24:15 "Choose."
   b. John 7:17 "will."
      1. NKJV "wills"
      2. ASV "willeth"
      3. NIV "chooses"
   c. Mt. 16:24 "will."
      1. NKJV "desires"
      2. The ASV and NIV have "would come."
      3. NIV "would"
   d. Rev. 22:17 "whosoever will,"
      1. "Whoever desires" NKJV
      2. "he that will" ASV
      3. "whoever wishes" NIV

C. **Word Meanings**
   1. **Predestine** (Predetermine) Romans 8:29,30; Ephesians 1: 5, 11
      a. This is the Greek word, "προορίζω" (prooridzoo).
      b. It means "that to which the subjects are predestined."
      c. It suggests that beforehand certain bounds, limitations, or criteria are set.
      d. "The question is **not who** are its objects, but **what** they are predestined to do"[1]

   2. **Elect/Election**
      a. The verb form is "ἐκλέγω" (eklegoo) meaning "to choose, pick out, select."
         1. It simply means the act of selecting or choosing one out of several options.

       2.   There is nothing to imply what is the basis for the choice.

    b.   The noun form is "ἐκλογή" (eklogay) meaning "a selection, a picking out."

3. **Foreknowledge**

    a.   The verb form is "προγινώσκω" (proginooskoo) meaning "to know before."

    b.   The noun form is "πρόγνωσις" (prognoosis) meaning "foreknowledge."

4. So, does the Bible teach "predestination," "election," and "foreknowledge?"

    a.   The answer is "ABSOLUTELY!"

    b.   A follow-up question is, "What does this "predestination" mean?

    c.   What are the **possible interpretations** that people might derive from the word "predestined?"

        1.   God has predetermined WHO will be saved by some arbitrary (to us) means, WHEN THEY WILL BE SAVED, and man has no say in the decision.

        2.   God has predetermined the conditions by which people can be saved. In order to become a part of the "elect" we must meet those conditions. The choice is ours.

    d.   So the real question is NOT "Does the Bible teach predestination?"; rather the real question is "What KIND of predestination does the Bible proclaim?"

5. Two Types Of Predestination:
    a. **"Individual Particular Election."**
        1. This is the idea that God, before the world began, chose specific individuals to save; it had nothing to do with any foreseen response on their part.
        2. **Arbitrary predestination** — no human involvement is required, it is not based on any reasoning we can determine or response we can give.
    b. **"Group Election."**
        1. This is the idea that God, because of His mercy or compassion extended grace or made a way whereby man could be saved. He PREDE-TERMINED A PLAN that those who desire to be saved would have to obey.
        2. **Criteria predestination** — people can choose to be a part of the "group" if the meet the predetermined criteria.
    c. Illustrations of **Particular** and **Group** election.
        1. Analogy of a **College course**:
            a. **Particular** — The teacher decides before the first class takes place that all students whose last names begin with B, G, K, P, T and W will get an "A." All other students will flunk.
                1. Implications:
                    a. There is nothing those not selected can do to get an "A."

b. There is nothing those selected can do (or not do) to not get an "A."

    a. They are sure to get an "A!"

    b. The students do not even know that they are selected to get an "A!"

2. How would you like to be in that class? Well, if your last name begins with B, G, K, P, T and W, it would be GREAT! What if it doesn't begin with those letters? You would be "TICKED OFF!"

b. **Group (Criteria)** — The teacher predetermines that all students whose point total for the semester is within 90% of the highest possible point total gets an "A."

1. Implications:

    a. Every student knows what is required to get an "A."

    b. Every student has the possibility of getting an "A."

    c. Every student has the possibility of NOT getting an "A."

2. It is a matter of talent, determination, and choice!

3. How would you like to be in THIS class?

c. Contrasts of these two types of election.

   1. Particular:

      a. The students have no responsibility.

      b. They have no control.

      c. They have no choice.

      d. The "A's" are only available to the chosen.

      e. It is not fair to everyone.

   2. Group:

      a. Students do have responsibility.

      b. They do have control.

      c. They do have choice.

      d. "A's" are available to all if they meet the criterion.

      e. It is fair to everyone.

2. Analogy of **sports playoffs**:

a. NFL Champions.

   1. **Particular** — It has been predetermined which team will win the Super Bowl before the season ever begins.

      a. The specific team has already been chosen.

      b. It does not matter how poorly they do or how well other teams do;

that team will win the Super Bowl.

2. **Group (Criteria)** — It is predetermined who will win the Super Bowl by the NFL.

   a. The specific team is not chosen!

   b. The winner of each of the wild card games, and divisional playoffs, and conference championships will play for the Super Bowl.

   c. The winner of the Super Bowl Game will be the NFL champions.

b. World Series Champions.

1. **Particular** — It has been predetermined which team will be the World Champions before the season ever begins.

   a. The specific team has already been chosen.

   b. It does not matter how poorly they do or how well other teams do; that team will win the World Series.

2. **Group (Criteria)** — Major League Baseball has predetermined who will win the World Series.

a. The winner of the 3 divisions in the American League and a wild card team, and the winner of the 3 divisions in the National League and a wild card team, will play to see who is the winner of the American League and who is the winner of the National League.

b. The winners of the American League and the National League will ultimately play in the World Series.

c. No, the New York Yankees or the Arizona Diamondbacks are NOT predetermined to be the champions!

3. Contrasts between Particular and Group election in salvation.

a. **Particular**:

1. Sinners have no responsibility.
2. They have no control.
3. They have no choice.
4. Salvation is only available to the chosen.
5. It is not fair to everyone; God is a "respecter of persons."

  b. **Group (Criteria)**:
    1. Sinners do have responsibility.
    2. They do have control.
    3. They do have choice.
    4. Salvation is available to all if they meet the criterion.
    5. It is fair to everyone; "God is no respecter of persons."
  c. The question is "Which of these two interpretations is consistent with Scripture? Which is correct?"

D. Context Of Passages
 1. **Ephesians 1:1-14**
  a. Who is Paul addressing? "the faithful in Christ Jesus" Verse 1
  b. **Does Paul identify any other criteria for election?**
    1. The place of salvation!
     a. **"In Him"** Verse 4
     b. In Christ and in His Church!
     c. That's the message of the book of Ephesians!
    2. The kind of life to be lived in salvation (once saved):
     a. "Holy and without blame before Him. Verse 4
     b. God expects the saved to live like they have been and are saved!
    3. Are there any actions that make up this criterion?

a. "**We** who first **trusted** in Christ" Verse 12

b. "In Him **you also trusted**, after you **heard** the word of truth...in whom also, having **believed**." Verse 13

c. Eph. 2:5,8,9

1. Verse 5: "Even when we were dead in sins, hath quickened us together with Christ, (by grace ye are saved;)"

2. Verse 8,9: "For **by grace** are ye saved **through faith**; and that not of yourselves: it is the gift of God: Not of works, lest any man should boast."

3. Grace: God's part!

4. Faith: Man's part!

5. The gift of God: salvation!

6. The Calvinist's interpretation of this passage:

a. Grace: God, the Father's gift.

b. Faith: God, the Holy Spirit's gift.

c. Gift: Faith is directly infused into the sinner by the Holy Spirit.

d. Thus they conclude man has NO responsibility.

2. **Romans 8:30**
   a. "Moreover whom he did **predestinate**, them he also **called**: and whom he called, them he also **justified**: and whom he justified, them he also **glorified**."
   b. Paul already described how we become justified.
      1. Rom. 3:26 "To declare, I say, at this time his righteousness: that he might be just, and the justifier of him which believeth in Jesus."
      2. "Belief in Jesus" involves a trust that submits to anything He asks!
      3. 8:28 "And we know that all things work together for good to them that love God, to them who are the called according to his purpose." The called are those who love God!
      4. And yes, it also involves baptism to get "into Christ!" Rom. 6:1-4
   c. Whose part is faith?
      1. Rom. 10:17 "So then faith cometh by hearing, and hearing by the word of God."
      2. The called have to hear the Word preached and believe it. Rom. 10:13-16

E. **Consistency With The Rest Of The Scriptures**
   1. To accept "Individual Particular Election", the arbitrary predestination view, will create a number of contradictions in the Scriptures!

2. God desires ALL men to be saved!
   a. I Tim. 2:3,4 "For this *is* good and acceptable in the sight of God our Saviour; **Who will have all men to be saved,** and to come unto the knowledge of the truth."
   b. II Pet. 3:9 "The Lord is not slack concerning his promise, as some men count slackness; but is longsuffering to us-ward, **not willing that any should perish, but that all should come to repentance.**"
   c. Heb. 2:9 "But we see Jesus, who was made a little lower than the angels for the suffering of death, crowned with glory and honour; that he by the grace of God should **taste death for every man.**"
   d. I Tim. 2: 6 "**Who gave himself a ransom for all,** to be testified in due time."
   e. I Jn. 2:2 "And he is the propitiation for our sins: and not for ours only, but also **for** *the sins of* **the whole world.**"
   f. Jn. 3:16 "For God so loved **the world,** that he gave his only begotten Son, that **whosoever** believeth in him should not perish, but have everlasting life."

3. God gives everyone CHOICE!
   a. Rev. 22:17 "And the Spirit and the bride say, Come. And let him that heareth say, Come. And let him that is athirst come. And **whosoever will,** let him take the water of life freely."
   b. Mt. 16:25 "For **whosoever will** save his life shall lose it: and **whosoever will** lose his life for my sake shall find it."

    c.   Mk. 8:34 "**Whosoever will** come after me, let him deny himself, and take up his cross, and follow me."

    d.   Heb. 5:8,9 "Though he were a Son, yet learned he obedience by the things which he suffered; And being made perfect, he became the author of eternal salvation **unto all them that obey him**;"

    e.   Jn. 3:16 "For God so loved the world, that he gave his only begotten Son, that **whosoever believeth** in him should not perish, but have everlasting life."

    f.   All of these verses suggest that "whoever desires to" may be saved!

4.   The Great Commission is an open invitation to any who will believe and obey!

    a.   Mt. 28:19 "Go ye therefore, and teach **all nations**, baptizing them in the name of the Father, and of the Son, and of the Holy Ghost:"

    b.   Mk. 16:15-16 "And he said unto them, Go ye into all the world, and preach the gospel to **every creature**. He that believeth and is baptized shall be saved; but he that believeth not shall be damned."

5.   God DID predestine and elect certain individuals for **specific roles or works**; but **NEVER for salvation**!

    a.   Rom. 9:11-13 God chose Jacob to carry on the Abrahamic promise instead of Esau!

    b.   Jn. 15:16 Christ chose the Apostles to that office!

      c.   God chose Paul to be an Apostle to the Gentiles! Ac. 9:15; 26:15-18

VI. Concluding Observations

A. Using The Teacher And Sports Analogies, Which View Seems More Consistent With God's Character?

B. Why Is The "Individual Particular Election" Or Arbitrary View Then So Popular?

    1. It removes all responsibility from man.

    2. If one is lost, it is GOD'S fault!

    3. Quote Of Calvinistic Statement About Predestination:

        a. "God's choice of certain individuals unto salvation before the foundation of the world rested solely in His own sovereign will. His choice of particular sinners was not based on any foreseen response or obedience on their part, such as faith, repentance, etc. On the contrary, God gives faith and repentance to each individual whom He selected. These acts are the result, not the cause of God's choice. Election therefore was not determined by or conditioned upon any virtuous quality or act foreseen in man. Those whom God sovereignly elected He brings through the power of the Spirit to a willing acceptance of Christ. Thus God's choice of the sinner, not the sinner's choice of Christ, is the ultimate cause of salvation."[2]

b. Observe the emphasis upon God determining which individuals will be saved and the declaration that God chooses and saves those He wills to be saved.

c. Also, observe the lack of ability for man to respond or to choose to be saved and the lack of responsibility of man to respond to God.

C. The Subjectivity Of "Individual Particular Election:"

1. How do you know you are on the list? YOU FEEL IT! It is pure subjectivity.

2. If you think you are on the list, then you have nothing to worry about?

D. Numerous Passages May Cause Much Confusion; They May Seem To Be Very Contradictory. However Study Confusing Passages In Light Of Passages That You Can Readily Grasp. Often This Helps Clarify Your Confusion Quickly.

Endnotes:

[1]Bullinger, E.W. *A Critical Lexicon and Concordance of the English and Greek New Testament*, Grand Rapids: Zondervan Publishing House, 1975, p. 597.

[2]Steele, David N. and Curtis C. Thomas. *The Five Points Of Calvinism: Defined, Defended, Documented,* Philadelphia: Presbyterian and Reformed Publishing Co, 1976, pp. 16,17.

Assignment:
- A. Texts: Ac. 2:16-21; Mt. 24:29,30

- B. Why Are These Passages "Difficult Passages?"

- C. Questions:
  1. At first glance, to what event do these passages seem to point?

  2. Do they refer to the same event?

  3. To what do these passages refer?

- D. What Tools Do You Need To Use To Solve This Problem?

Figurative Language

Introduction:
- A. Literal Language Can Be Immediately Interpreted Without Major Study.

- B. Figurative Language Demands More Intensive Investigation.

- C. The Goal Of This Lesson: To Learn How To Distinguish And To Interpret Literal And Figurative Language.

I. **Texts: Acts 2:16-21; Matthew 24:29-30**

II. **The Problem:**
- A. What Type Of Literature Is In Our Texts?
  1. Literal?

  2. Figurative?

- B. **If LITERAL, To What Do These Verses Refer?**
  1. Realize how quickly a literal interpretation can make us go "brain dead!"

2. If one just assumes that these Scriptures are literal without thinking further, what will he immediately conclude? He will be convinced that these passages refer to THE END OF THE WORLD!

C. **If FIGURATIVE,** To What Do They Refer?

D. Do Both Passages Refer To The Same Event?

III. **What Tools Can We Use In Solving This Problem?**
   A. **Understand The Difference Between Literal And Figurative Context.**

   B. Study The **Immediate Context.**

   C. Study **O.T. Prophecies And Fulfillments.**

   D. Study **O.T. Usage Of Such Language.**

   E. Consider **The Consequences Of Using The Wrong Interpretation.**

IV. **Using Our Tools To Solve The Problem.**
   A. **Understand The Difference Between Literal And Figurative Context. Guidelines And Dangers In Interpreting Literal And Figurative Language!**
      1. **Guidelines:**
         a. **In general, we should interpret scriptures literally.**
            1. This is the same approach we use when reading ordinary books like a history book or a manual for using a newly purchased item.
               a. Read a brief passage from a history book.
                  1. Dec. 16, 1773 "On the evening of the 16th some 8,000 people assembled in and near Boston's Old South church heard Capt. Rotch of the *Dartmouth* inform Sam Adams, chairman of the meeting, of the Governor's final refusal. Thereupon, at a signal from Adams, a disciplined group of men disguised as Mohawk Indians rushed to Griffin's Wharf, boarded the tea ships, and, working through the night, dumped all the tea (342 chests) into the harbor. No other property aboard was damaged."[1]
                  2. Do you approach such history literally or

figuratively? Obviously literally!

b. Read a brief instruction from a manual for a household product.

1. In our office we purchased an AT&T Digital Answering Machine with mailboxes. Concerning the mailbox use the manual states, "This answering system offers three voice mailboxes, providing a convenient way to share an answering system with other members of your household or business. Callers using a touch tone phone can select the mailbox in which their messages will be recorded by pressing 1,2 or 3 after the system answers the call. Those not using a touch tone phone, or those who do not press 1,2 or 3, can still leave a message, which is automatically recorded in Mailbox 1."[2]

2. Do you approach such instructions literally or figuratively? Obviously literally!

2. The Bible deals with the literal world, real people, real events, and real doctrine.

        3. Therefore, always begin by attempting to interpret a passage literally.

  b. **Interpret the scripture as figurative under the following conditions**:

      1. If a literal interpretation involves an impossibility.

          a. Jesus stating that He is the door, Jn. 10:7,9

          b. Jesus affirming that He is the vine and Christians are the branches, Jn. 15:1-6.

      2. If a literal interpretation makes the Bible contradict itself.

          a. David's use of hyperbole in Ps. 51:5 when compared to Ps. 8:5,6 and Ezek. 18:4,20.

          b. David's use of hyperbole in Ps. 22:6 when compared to Ps. 8:5,6 and Gen. 1:26,27.

      3. If a literal interpretation demands actions that are wrong. "Pluck out eye or cut off hand." Mt. 5:29,30 when compared to I Cor. 6:15-20.

      4. When it is put in a form that makes it obviously figurative (Example: mockery).

          a. Gal. 5:12 (See 2c2 below)

          b. Js. 2:19 "Thou believest that there is one God; **thou doest well**: the devils also believe, and tremble." James is using sarcasm. "Whoopee!" "Big deal!"

c. **Remember that just because a word is used figuratively in one place does not mean that it is always used figuratively!**
    1. "Door"
        a. Literal: Mt. 27:60
        b. Figurative: Jn. 10:7,9
    2. "Lamb"
        a. Literal: Ex. 12:3-5
        b. Figurative: Jn. 1:29,36
    3. "Word"
        a. Literal: Mt. 4:4
        b. Figurative: Jn. 1:1,14

2. **Dangers:**
    a. **Be careful not to apply passages to all people if it was intended only for one person or a few people!**
        1. Mt. 10:9,10 "Get you no gold, nor silver, nor brass in your purses; [10]no wallet for *your* journey, neither two coats, nor shoes, nor staff: for the laborer is worthy of his food." ASV
        2. Mk. 6:8,9 "And commanded them that they should **take nothing for** *their* **journey, save a staff only**; no scrip, no bread, no money in *their* purse: [9]But *be* shod with sandals; and not put on two coats."
        3. This was spoken only to the 12 on the "Limited Commission." Mt. 10:5,6; Mk. 6:7
        4. Jesus was telling the Apostles that they would be cared for or receive the provisions they needed as they went.

5. This is not telling every Christian to just get up, go journey to teach the lost, and take no provisions.
6. Another example involves the promises of the Holy Spirit and His guidance to the Apostles. Jn. 14:26; 15:26; 16:13

b. **Be careful not to interpret literal events or truths as being figurative!**
    1. Why?
    2. You will completely miss monumental truths!
    3. The Creation account, parting of the Red Sea, Jesus miracles, and the Resurrection are NOT figurative! They are literal events!
    4. To attempt to make them figurative would be to rob them of their genuineness and import!

c. **Be careful not to interpret figurative events or truths as literal!**
    1. "I am a worm, and no man." Ps. 22:6. Was David a literal "worm?"
    2. "I would they were even cut off which trouble you." Gal. 5:12
        a. ASV "I would that they that unsettle you would even go beyond circumcision."
        b. NIV "As for those agitators, I wish they would go the whole way and emasculate themselves!"
        c. The Greek word "ἀποκόψονται" (apokopsontai) means "to cut off from," "to amputate," (by irony)

to mutilate (the private parts).

d. This is a figurative statement stated in irony as Paul discusses the "circumcised" who were causing so many problems for Gentile Christians. He wishes that they were not only circumcised; he wished they would even be mutilated or castrated.

e. Was Paul advocating emasculation of the body? Obviously not!

f. Paul wished that the Judaizing teachers would not only circumcise themselves but would completely castrate themselves; he wished that these false teachers would completely cut themselves off from hindering these brethren.

3. Jesus is not a literal "door" (Jn. 10:9) or a literal "vine" (Jn. 15:1).

4. Today's verses:

a. If we misapply them, we completely miss the whole point of these passages.

b. When we apply them to the end of the world, we miss everything Jesus was saying.

d. **Be careful not to attach doctrine to something meant figuratively**.

1. A literal interpretation of Rev. 20 was largely responsible for the promotion of the doctrine of premillenialism.

2.   Ps. 51:5   David used hyperbole to express the painful guilt he felt; Calvinists use this passage to advocate "original sin."

B. **The Immediate Context: Acts 2:16-21**
1.   What is the **context** of this passage?
   a.   This is on the Day of Pentecost, the day the Plan of Salvation was first presented and people were invited into the Church.
   b.   Those observing the Apostles speaking in foreign languages were asking, "What is going on?"
   c.   Peter explains what is happening! 14-21

2.   What are some **possible solutions or possible interpretations** of verses 19,20?
   a.   The **Judgment Day**. (This is likely the first answer one contemplates!)
   b.   The **Destruction of Jerusalem**.
   c.   The **Day of Pentecost**; arrival of the Church.
   d.   The **Period From Pentecost to Judgment**.
   e.   The **end of the Law Of Moses**.

3.   **Evaluation of the possible solutions**.
   a.   **The Judgment Day**.
      1.   If one concludes this is the proper interpretation, he will immediately stop thinking.
      2.   This interpretation contradicts Peter's inspired explanation in verse 16 "But **this is that which** was spoken by the prophet Joel."

        3.   One might decide that the miraculous gifts would last until the Judgment Day.

  b. **The Destruction of Jerusalem**.

        1.   Would this affirm that the miraculous would end by A.D. 70?

        2.   One is then forced to conclude that the entire Bible was written before that date.

        3.   The Holy Spirit continued to impart spiritual gifts after A.D. 70; He gave the Apostle John the gift of prophecy as he wrote the Gospel of John, I, II, III John, and Revelation. A.D. 93-96

  c. **The Day of Pentecost**.

        1.   This would seem to suggest that these miracles would only occur on that day.

        2.   But note the promise, "I will pour out of my Spirit upon all flesh:"

        3.   Acts 10 proves that is not true; the Gospel was then taken to the Gentiles; they received miraculous gifts.

  d. **The period from Pentecost to Judgment**.

        1.   This would promote the Pentecostal interpretation.

        2.   One would hold the view that the miraculous gifts would last until the Judgment Day.

  e. **The end of the Law Of Moses**.

        1.   This would demand a figurative interpretation.

        2.   The former Law, the Law of Moses, had been abolished.

4. **Solution.**
   a. **"This is that"**
      1. Compare the immediate statements to their original prophecy!
      2. What O.T. prophecy is quoted?
      3. This is a fulfillment of **Joel's prophecy in Joel 2:28-32**.
      4. Then Peter quoted Joel's prophecy.
      5. **Verses 17,18 are LITERAL!**
         a. Joel was declaring that the Holy Spirit would give gifts to those under the New Covenant; believers would prophesy; they would receive dreams and visions.
         b. This was a fulfillment of Jesus' prophecy in Mk. 16:17,18
         c. This occurred as the Apostles laid hands on believers. Ac. 6:1-6; 8:5-23
         d. "All flesh" included the Jewish Christians (Ac. 2-9) and Gentile Christians (Ac. 10; I Cor. 12-14; Rom. 1:11).
   b. **Interpreting verses 19,20:**
      1. A literal interpretation would have these verses referring to the "End of the World."
         a. At first glance this may seem very plausible.
         b. However, the "This is that" of verse 16 proves this is not talking about the "End of the World!"

2. If this passage is not to be interpreted literally, then to what does it refer figuratively?

3. **This is an example of O.T. apocalyptic language and its figurative nature!**

   a. It is used to describe the fall or end of a great nation or something that has been firmly established and is about to be removed.

   b. Examples:
      1. Is. 13:1,6,10,13 Refers to the fall of **Babylon**.
      2. Is. 19:1 Refers to the fall of **Egypt**.
      3. Is. 23:17,12; 24:19-23 Refers to the fall of **Tyre**.
      4. Is. 34:4,5 Refers to the fall of **Israel's enemies**.
      5. Ezek. 32:2,6-8 Refers to the fall of **Egypt**.
      6. Joel 2:1,10,31 God's judgment coming upon **Judah**.
      7. Daniel 7:11-13 Fall of the four beast representing four empires: **Babylon, Medo-Persia, Greece, and Rome**.
      8. Amos 8:9 Refers to the fall of **Israel**.

   c. **Verses 19,20 are FIGURATIVE!**
      1. **Why would apocalyptic language be used here?**
      2. What would it have meant to this Jewish audience?

3. To what could Joel have been prophesying and Peter was now declaring that had been done away?
4. Answer:
   a. They knew that Jeremiah had prophesied that the Jews would be given a NEW Law! Jer. 31:31-34
   b. They knew a Messiah was prophesied.
   c. Peter's whole sermon is: Jesus is the Messiah; the New Covenant is now here!
   d. Thus, the Law of Moses, what the Jews saw as their very foundation, has been removed!
5. Present-day examples of using figurative language that is very expressive.
   a. "Custer's last stand" (to figuratively express hopeless-ness).
   b. "Attila the Hun" (to figuratively describe a ruthless, barbaric, angry, tyrannical person such as a boss).

C. **The Immediate Context: Mt. 24:29-31**
   1. What is the **context** of this passage?
      a. Jesus is talking to His Apostles about the destruction of the Temple and the surrounding buildings. 1,2

    b.   The disciples ask three questions. 3
        1.   "Tell us, when shall these things be?" When will the Temple be destroyed?
        2.   "What shall be the sign of thy coming?"
        3.   "When will the end of the world occur?"
        4.   Obviously they assumed that these events would occur simultaneously at the end of the world.

2.   What are some **possible solutions or possible interpretations of Mt. 24:29-31**?
    a.   The **Judgment Day**. (This is likely the first answer one contemplates!)
    b.   The **Day of Pentecost; arrival of the Church**.
    c.   The **end of the Law Of Moses**.
    d.   The **Destruction of Jerusalem**.

3.   **Evaluation of the possible solutions.**
    a.   **The Judgment Day**.
        1.   If one concludes this is the proper interpretation, he will immediately stop thinking.
        2.   This interpretation contradicts Jesus' explanations:
            a.   That signs will point to this event.
            b.   That the message is for those who live in Judea. 16
            c.   That "This generation shall not pass, till all these things be fulfilled." 34

b. **The Day of Pentecost; the arrival of the Church.**
  1. There is no historical record of all the tribulations that Jesus mentioned occurring just before the Day of Pentecost in Ac. 2.
  2. The Gospel had not been preached at all before that Day. 14

c. **The end of the Law Of Moses.**
  1. That was going to occur when Jesus died on the Cross. Eph. 2:15; Col. 2:14
  2. Jesus spoke the prophecy of Matthew 24 on Tuesday just before His Crucifixion on Friday.
  3. There is simply no time for all of the signs to occur that He has prophesied.
  4. The Temple still stood after His Death!

d. **The Destruction of Jerusalem.**
  1. Jesus is pointing to the decimation of the influence of Judaism.
  2. It would be such a "thorn in the side" of the Church; however, the Temple would be destroyed and Judaism's influence would wane.

4. **Solution:**
  a. **In the immediate context, Jesus talks about the Fall of Jerusalem and the signs that point to it!** 4-28
    1. **The signs:**
      a. Deceivers. 5
      b. Wars and rumors of wars. 6

        c.   Famines, pestilences, and earthquakes. 7

        d.   False prophets. 11

        e.   The love of many disciples will wane. 12

        f.   The Gospel will be preached to the whole world. 14

        g.   When "the abomination of desolation" is seen, the disciples are to flee to the mountains of Judea. 15,16

            1.   Lk. 21:20

            2.   Armies surrounding Jerusalem.

    2.   All these signs were to occur before Jerusalem fell.

  b. **Specific phrases that give insight and assist in interpreting this chapter**.

    1.   Verses 4-35 Refer to the Signs pointing to the Fall of Jerusalem.

        a.   **"Those days"** 19,22

        b.   **"These things"** 6,33,34

        c.   **"This generation"** 34

    2.   Verses 36-51 along with chapter 25 describe the Judgment Day.

        a.   **"That day"** 36

        b.   **"That hour"** 36,42,44,50

        c.   **"As the days of Noah were"** 37,38 NO SIGNS

  c. If our text IS figurative, to what does it refer?

    1.   The destruction of Jerusalem would bring a **death nail to Judaism and Jewish culture**.

2. Their very spiritual foundation would be destroyed.
   a. They had NO Temple!
   b. They had NO genealogical records; they were all destroyed.
   c. They had NO priesthood; again the records were all destroyed.
3. It will occur within "this generation." 34
   a. A Bible generation is 40 years.
   b. Jesus is declaring that it would occur within the next 40 years!
   c. It happened in 33 years.
   d. If it has not occurred today, there must be some people who are about 2,000 years old still living!
4. There would be "signs" of the Fall of Jerusalem; however there will be NO signs about the Lord's Second Coming. Therefore continual preparation is of utmost importance.

Conclusion:
A. These Texts Illustrate How We Must Be Careful Before We Just Assume That A Passage Is Literal.

B. Just Be Cautious To Take Time And Make Sure How Language Is Being Used In Passages Before You Come To A Firm Decision About Its Meaning.

Endnotes

[1]*Encyclopedia of American History*, editor: Richard B. Morris, Harper & Row, New York, NY. 1965. p. 81.

[2]*AT&T 1726 Digital Answering System With Mailboxes*; China; 953W120001D0000; 09,01.

Assignment:
A. Observe Different Usages Of The Same Word In Scripture.

B. The Words:
1. **"Tradition"**: II Thess. 2:15; 3:6; Mt. 15:5:6; Mk. 7:9,13; Col. 2:8

2. **"Desire"**: I Cor. 14:1; I Cor. 12:31; 14:39; Ac. 7:9; 13:45; 17:5

3. **"Mark"**: Lk. 11:35, Phil. 2:4; 3:17, II Cor. 4:18, Gal. 6:1; Rom. 16:17

4. **"Church"**: Mt. 16:18; Ac. 8:1,3; 11:26; 20:28; Eph. 1:22,23; 3:10; 5:25; I Tim. 3:15; Ac. 19:32,39,41

5. **"Elder"**: I Tim. 5:19; I Pet. 5:1; Tit. 2:2,3; I Tim. 5:1

6. **"Deacon"**: Phil. 1:1; I Tim. 3:8,10,12,13; Rom. 16:1

C.   What Is The Problem?

D.   How Do You Solve The Problem?

E.   What Important Principle Do You Learn From This Lesson?

Lesson Eleven

Different Usage Of Words

Introduction:

   A. Texts:

      1. **"Tradition"**: II Thess. 2:15; 3:6; Mt. 15:5:6; Mk. 7:9,13; Col. 2:8

      2. **"Desire"**: I Cor. 14:1; I Cor. 12:31; 14:39; Ac. 7:9; 13:45; 17:5

      3. **"Mark"**: Lk. 11:35, Phil. 2:4; 3:17, II Cor. 4:18, Gal. 6:1; Rom. 16:17

      4. **"Church"**: Mt. 16:18; Ac. 8:1,3; 11:26; 20:28; Eph. 1:22,23; 3:10; 5:25; I Tim. 3:15; Ac. 19:32,39,41

      5. **"Elder"**: I Tim. 5:19; I Pet. 5:1; Tit. 2:2,3; I Tim. 5:1

      6. **"Deacon"**: Phil. 1:1; I Tim. 3:8,10,12,13; Rom. 16:1

   B. Observe Different Usages Of These Words.

   C. This Lesson Today Is Not A Study Of A Specific Text As Other Lessons Are.

      1. It is more conceptual.

2. Many of the tools that we have used in other lessons will not be helpful in this lesson; however, some tools will be very helpful.

D. Examples Of Words That Have General And Specific Meanings:
   1. "Truck"
      a. General usage: vehicles that are more rugged than a car.
         1. Any kind of truck.
         2. Toy truck.
         3. SUV.
         4. Pickup.
         5. Semi; tractor and trailer.
      b. Specific usage:
         1. A large vehicle that hauls cargo.
         2. A tractor and trailer.

   2. "Coke"
      a. General Usage: Any kind of soft drink.
      b. Specific Usage: Coca Cola.

E. Examples Of Words That May Have Positive And Negative Meanings.
   1. Two types of approaches to words.
      a. Denotative — the dictionary definition.
      b. Connotative – the emotional reaction of the person who hears the word.

   2. Example:
      a. "Cat"
         1. Denotative meaning:

        a. A feline.

        b. A 4-legged mammal with whiskers that is often tamed to stay in people's houses.

        c. A live mouse trap.

    2. Connotative meaning:

        a. To cat owners — warm, loveable pets.

        b. To others — independent, sneaky animal.

        c. To those allergic to cats — runny nose and eyes, itchy eyes and neck, and sneezing.

  b. "Snake"

    1. Denotative meaning:

        a. A reptile.

        b. A long slithering and often dangerous reptile.

    2. Connotative meaning:

        a. To some manufacturers — skins used to make different items.

        b. To most people, a slithery, scary, and feared reptile.

        c. Many immediately think of Satan because he used the serpent to deceived Eve in the Garden of Eden.

I. **The Problem:**

  A. The Same Word Often Can Have Different Meanings And Connotations; One Use May Be Negative, Another Use May Be Positive.

B. Too, The Same Word Can Be Used In A General Sense Or It Can Also Be Used In A Very Technical Specific Sense.

C. This Demands That As We Be Careful Before We Quickly Conclude That A Word Is Defined In A Certain Way.

II. What Tools Can We Use In Solving This Problem?
A. **Context!**

B. **Concordances** To See Where These Words Are Used Throughout Scripture.

C. **Word Studies** To Understand The Root Meaning Of The Words.

III. Using Our Tools To Solve The Problem: Words That Have Both Negative And Positive Meanings.
A. **"Tradition"**: II Thess. 2:15; 3:6; Mt. 15:5:6; Mk. 7:9,13;Col. 2:8
   1. Definitions:
      a. The word **"παράδοσις"** (paradosis) typically means "something handed down." This word has no inherent negative or positive connotation.
      b. The question is: "How is the word being used in its context? Negatively? Or "Positively?"

    c.   Looking up the words in a concordance or in the Greek language will be of NO help! Context will be the determining factor!

2. **"Tradition" that is condemned. ("Negative tradition.")**

    a.   This use of "tradition" involves following men's teachings and practices; it includes doing things contrary to God's revealed Will.

    b.   Mt. 15:6 "Thus have ye made the commandment of God of none effect by your **tradition**."

    c.   Mk. 7:9 "Full well ye reject the commandment of God, that ye may keep your own **tradition**."

    d.   Mk. 7:13 "Making the word of God of none effect through your **tradition**, which ye have delivered: and many such like things do ye."

    e.   Col. 2:8 "Beware lest any man spoil you through philosophy and vain deceit, after the **tradition** of men, after the rudiments of the world, and not after Christ."

    f.   Condemned "tradition" involves following the commandments of men.

        1.   Mt. 15:9 "But in vain they do worship me, teaching *for* doctrines the commandments of men."

        2.   The Pharisees were condemned for their "tradition;" this was exalting THEIR WILL to an equal position with (or one above) the Law of Moses.

3. **"Tradition" that is condoned. ("Condoned tradition.")**

   a. I Cor. 11:2 "Now I praise you, brethren, that ye remember me in all things, and keep the **ordinances,** as I delivered *them* to you.."

   b. II Thess. 2:15 "Therefore, brethren, stand fast, and hold the **traditions** which ye have been taught, whether **by word,** or **our epistle."**

   c. II Thess. 3:6 "Now we command you, brethren, in the name of our Lord Jesus Christ, that ye withdraw yourselves from every brother that walketh disorderly, and not after the **tradition** which he received of us."

4. **"Condemned tradition"** is worshiping and teaching men's opinions or our own ideas; **"Condoned tradition"** is following what the Apostles and Prophets have received by revelation and have declared unto mankind, whether by oral proclamation or by inspired letter.

B. **"Desire":** I Cor. 14:1; I Cor. 12:31; 14:39; Ac. 7:9; 13:45; 17:5

   1. ' The Greek word **"ζηλόω"** (dzaylooo) refers to "strong desire."

      a. This word has no inherent negative or positive connotations.

      b. The same Greek word is used in all of the above verses.

    c. However, when you hear the word "covet" or "strong desire" what connotative meaning do you immediately have?

       1. Negative or positive?

       2. Most students associate the word covet with the 10th Commandment, "Thou shalt not covet." Ex. 20:17

2. The question is: "How is the word being used in its context? Negatively? Or "Positively?"

3. Again, looking up the words in a concordance or in the Greek language will be of NO help! Context will be the determining factor!

4. In its **negative sense**, "ζηλόω" (dzaylooo) refers to being envious.

    a. Ac. 7:9 "And the patriarchs, moved with **envy**, sold Joseph into Egypt: but God was with him,"

    b. Ac. 13:45 "But when the Jews saw the multitudes, they were filled with **envy**, and spake against those things which were spoken by Paul, contradicting and blaspheming."

    c. Ac. 17:5 "But the Jews which believed not, moved with **envy**, took unto them certain lewd fellows of the baser sort, and gathered a company, and set all the city on an uproar, and assaulted the house of Jason, and sought to bring them out to the people."

    5.   In its **positive sense**, "ζηλόω" (dzayloo) refers to intense desire to do good.

        a.   I Cor. 12:31 "But **covet** earnestly the best gifts:"

        b.   I Cor. 14:1 "Follow after charity, and **desire** spiritual *gifts*, but rather that ye may prophesy."

        c.   I Cor. 14:39 "Wherefore, brethren, **covet** to prophesy, and forbid not to speak with tongues."

C.   **"Mark"**: Lk. 11:35, Phil. 2:4; 3:17, II Cor. 4:18, Gal. 6:1; Rom. 16:17

    1.   This is the Greek word "σκοπεῖν" (skopein) which means "watch, observe, to take note of. This is what a banker or businessman does about one who will not pay his bills.

        a.   This word also has no inherent negative or positive connotations.

        b.   The same Greek word is used in all of the above verses.

        c.   However, when you hear the word "mark" what connotative meaning do you immediately have?

            1.   Negative or positive?

            2.   Most students associate the word "mark" connotatively in a negative way because they relate it with sinful brethren being "marked."

    2.   The question is: "How is the word being used in its context? Negatively? Or "Positively?"

3. Again, looking up the words in a concordance or in the Greek language will be of NO help! Context will be the determining factor!

4. It is used in a **negative sense** of watching for danger.
   a. Watch for danger: Rom. 16:17
   b. Take note of those who cause divisions.
      1. This is the Greek word "διχοστασίας" (dichostasias).
      2. It is also used in Gal. 5:20 and translated "seditions."
      3. It means "dissensions, divisions, disunions, causing trouble among brethren."
   c. Those who cause "offenses."
      1. This is the Greek word "σκάνδαλα" (scandala); this is the source of the English word "scandal."
      2. It means "stumblingblocks" or "causes of indignation."
   d. How should such divisive brethren be treated? "Avoid them."
   e. This same usage is in Lk. 11:35, "Watch lest the light in you become darkness."

5. It is used in a **positive sense** of watching for godly living that you can imitate.
   a. Watch for godly living you can imitate. Phil. 3:17
      1. KJV "Brethren, be followers together of me, and **mark** them which walk so as ye have us for an ensample."
      2. NKJV "Brethren, join in following

         my example, and **note** those who so walk, as you have us for a pattern."
3. NIV "Join with others in following my example, brothers, and **take note of** those who live according to the pattern we gave you."
  b. Be watchful:
    1. In order to make a wise decision. II Cor. 4:18
    2. As you try to restore brethren from their sin. Do not allow yourself to be tempted and go into sin yourself. Gal. 6:1
    3. To see others needs more than dwelling upon your own needs. In doing so, imitate Christ! Phil. 2:4

IV. Using Our Tools To Solve The Problem: Words That Are Used In Different Senses; Both General And Specific.
  A. "**Church**": Mt. 16:18; Ac. 8:1,3; 11:26; 20:28; Eph. 1:22,23; 3:10; 5:25; I Tim. 3:15; Ac. 19:32,39,41
    1. The Greek word "ἐκκλησία" (ekklaysia) translated "church" refers to any assembly that is "called out,"

    2. In its **general sense,** "ἐκκλησία" (ekklaysia) refers to any group "called out" for any reason. It may even refer to a mob or a convened court!

    a.   Mob.
        1.   Ac. 19:32 "Some therefore cried one thing, and some another: for the **assembly** was confused; and the more part knew not wherefore they were come together."
        2.   Ac. 19:41 "And when he had thus spoken, he dismissed the **assembly**."
    b.   A convened court or legal proceding: Ac. 19:39 "But if ye inquire any thing concerning other matters, it shall be determined in a lawful **assembly**."

3.   In its **specific sense**, "**ἐκκλησία**" (ekklaysia) refers to those who are the called out," those who have listened to the Lord's call, who have left sin, and who have to Him for salvation.
    a.   Mt. 16:18 "And I say also unto thee, That thou art Peter, and upon this rock I will build my **church**; and the gates of hell shall not prevail against it."
    b.   Ac. 8:1,3 "And Saul was consenting unto his death. And at that time there was a great persecution against the **church** which was at Jerusalem; and they were all scattered abroad throughout the regions of Judaea and Samaria, except the apostles....As for Saul, he made havock of the **church**, entering into every house, and haling men and women committed *them* to prison."
    c.   Ac. 11:26 "And when he had found him, he brought him unto Antioch. And it came to pass, that a whole year they assembled themselves with the **church**,

and taught much people. And the disciples were called Christians first in Antioch."

d.   Ac. 20:28 "Take heed therefore unto yourselves, and to all the flock, over the which the Holy Ghost hath made you overseers, to feed the **church** of God, which he hath purchased with his own blood."

e.   Eph. 1:22,23 "And hath put all *things* under his feet, and gave him *to be* the head over all *things* to the **church**, ²³Which is his body, the fulness of him that filleth all in all."

f.   Eph. 3:10 "To the intent that now unto the principalities and powers in heavenly *places* might be known by the **church** the manifold wisdom of God,"

g.   Eph. 5:25 "Husbands, love your wives, even as Christ also loved the **church**, and gave himself for it;"

h.   I Tim. 3:15 "But if I tarry long, that thou mayest know how thou oughtest to behave thyself in the house of God, which is the **church** of the living God, the pillar and ground of the truth."

B.   **"Elder"**: I Tim. 5:19; I Pet. 5:1; Tit. 2:2,3; I Tim. 5:1
   1.   Similarly, the word "πρεσβύτερος" (presbuteros) is used in a general sense and in a specific sense.

   2.   In its **general sense** "elder" refers to an older person, whether male or female.

    a.   Tit. 2:2 "That the **aged men** be sober, grave, temperate, sound in faith, in charity, in patience."

    b.   I Tim. 5:1 "Rebuke not an **elder**, but entreat *him* as a father; *and* the younger men as brethren;"

    c.   The word is also used in the feminine sense. Tit. 2:3 "The **aged women** likewise, that *they be* in behaviour as becometh holiness, not false accusers, not given to much wine, teachers of good things;"

3.   In a **specific sense**, "πρεσβύτερος" (presbuteros) designates men who are the shepherds who oversee the work of the local congregation.

    a.   I Tim. 5:19 "Against an **elder** receive not an accusation, but before two or three witnesses."

    b.   I Pet. 5:1 "The **elders** which are among you I exhort, who am also an elder, and a witness of the sufferings of Christ, and also a partaker of the glory that shall be revealed:"

    c.   They are also identified as "bishops" and "shepherds." I Tim. 3:1-7; Phil. 1:1; Ac. 20:17,28-30.

C.   "**Deacon**": Phil. 1:1; I Tim. 3:8,10,12,13; Rom. 16:1

1.   Similarly, the word "διάκονος" (diakonos) is used in a general sense and in a specific sense. The word is transliterated in English "**deacon**".

2. It is used in a **general sense** to describe anyone who serves or ministers to others.

    a. Rom. 16:1 Phoebe. "I commend unto you Phoebe our sister, which is a **servant** of the church which is at Cenchrea:"

    b. This passage has been used to defend:

        1. Women leading prayer in mixed Bible study groups.

        2. Women leading prayer in worship.

        3. Women leading singing in worship (often in groups called "Praise Teams").

        4. Women waiting on the Lord's Table.

        5. Women teaching the Bible in classes made up of male and female Christians.

        6. Appointing women as deacons or elders in congregations.

    c. Study of the **immediate text** and the **extended N.T. context**!

        1. The immediate context:

            a. Phoebe was a servant of the church at Cenchrea.

            b. She had become a "succourer" of many, and of myself also. KJV

                1. ASV: "helper of many,"

                2. NIV: "she has been a great help to many people,"

                3. The word here can mean "patron" or one who is a protector or a supporter (oftentimes it means a financial supporter).

a. Sometimes it is used on one leading.
   1. Rom. 12:8 "ruleth"
   2. I Thess. 5:12 "over you in the Lord."
   3. Elders must be those "that ruleth well his own house." I Tim. 3:5
   4. Deacons must also. I Tim. 3:12
   5. Elders who rule well should be counted worthy of double honour. I Tim. 5:17
b. Sometimes it is used of one diligently practicing good works. Tit. 3:8,14.
   1. This is the idea of meeting needs that arise.
   2. This seems to be what is suggested here about Phoebe.
c. Lk. 8:1-3 gives an illustration of other women who are described as "ministering" to Jesus.
   1. "And it came to pass afterward, that he went throughout every city and village, preaching and showing the glad

tidings of the kingdom of God: and the twelve *were* with him, [2]And certain women, which had been healed of evil spirits and infirmities, Mary called Magdalene, out of whom went seven devils, [3]And Joanna the wife of Chuza Herod's steward, and Susanna, and many others, which ministered unto him of their substance."

2. "Ministered" is the Greek word "διηκόνουν" (diaykonoun).

3. They gave of their possessions to assist Jesus and the Apostles to teach the word.

2. The extended N.T. context:

a. First, having God-ordained roles is NOT a castigation or vilification of women!

1. It is not a suggestion about any woman's ability, morality, spirituality, or quality.

2. God's choice of Mary to the elevated position of being the mother of the Messiah

certainly exemplifies His respect for women!

3. All Christians, male and female are "one" in Christ!
    a. Gal. 3:28 "There is neither Jew nor Greek, there is neither bond nor free, there is neither male nor female: for ye are all one in Christ Jesus."
    b. This verse must be studied contextually.
    c. Every human being is given the opportunity to come to salvation at the point of baptism, verse 27, and to live the Christian life as a child of God by faith in Christ Jesus, verse 26.
    d. The privilege to be a Christian is for everyone, Jew or Greek, slave or freeman, male or female.
    e. However, this passage does NOT address different roles.
4. God has given husbands and wives different roles in the home. Eph. 5:22-33
5. God has given men and women different roles in the Church.

a. I Tim. 2:1-15
b. I Cor. 14:34,35

6. These different roles are no more a castigation or vilification of women than the submission of Christ to the headship of God the Father is a castigation or vilification of Him! I Cor. 11:3 "But I would have you know, that the head of every man is Christ; and the head of the woman *is* the man; and the head of Christ *is* God."

b. Second, God has given men leadership roles in the home and in the Church.

1. In the home:
   a. The husband is to be the head of the home. Eph. 5:23
   b. This is neither a tyrannical headship nor a dictatorship.
   c. It is a loving, caring, understanding, compassionate leadership. Eph. 5:25,28,33

2. In the church, men are given the God-ordained role of leadership. I Tim. 2:8-15
   a. Elders are to be the bishops or overseers of the work of the church.

    b.   Similarly, as in the home, it is to be a loving, caring, understanding, compassionate leadership. I Pet. 5:1-3

  c. These roles are not culturally dictated; they are bound by God from the Creation.

    1. The male and female roles were in effect at the Creation; they were, in fact, strengthened after Eve so readily succumbed to Satan's devious temptation. Gen. 2:18; 3:1-8,16; I Tim. 2:11-15

    2. The Corinthian women mistakenly assumed that if they were "free in Christ," I Cor. 8-10, then they were also free to throw off the veil, a sign of submission to male leadership.

    3. Paul's inspired answer was that male headship was established by God at the Creation; Christians must not have any tradition that contradicts God's Word! I Cor. 11:1-16

  d. Some also use I Tim. 3:11 "Even so *must their* wives *be* grave, not slanderers, sober, faithful in all things" to claim that this refers to "deaconesses."

1. This is not good interpretation.
2. Why?
   a. Elders and deacons must be the "husband of one wife."
   b. Both must have faithful wives and they must have children.
   c. Elders must have "believing children (Christians).
   d. Deacons must have children.
   e. If this passage refers to "deaconesses", they do not have to be married or have children. There is no qualification about their marital or motherly status.
   f. BUT, if this passage refers to the wives of elders and deacons, then the qualifications about being wives and mothers has already been addressed!

3. The larger Biblical context shows that the word "διάκονος" (diakonos) is used in a **specific sense** to refer to men who are qualified servants who assist the elders in ministering to the congregation.
   a. Phil. 1:1 "Paul and Timotheus, the servants of Jesus Christ, to all the saints in Christ Jesus which are at Philippi, with the bishops and **deacons**:"
   b. I Tim. 3:
      1. 8 "Likewise *must* the **deacons** *be* grave, not doubletongued, not given to much wine, not greedy of filthy lucre;"

2. 10 "And let these also first be proved; then let them use the office of a **deacon**, being *found* blameless.."
3. 12 "Let the **deacons** be the husbands of one wife, ruling their children and their own houses well."
4. 13 "For they that have used the office of a **deacon** well purchase to themselves a good degree, and great boldness in the faith which is in Christ Jesus."

V. Conclusion:

A. Again, Before Jumping To An Immediate Decision As To What A Word Means, Be Sure To Look At The Context.

B. Remember:
   1. Some words are used in both a negative and in a positive sense.

   2. Some words are used in a general sense and in a technical spiritual sense.

C. Always Keep The Context In Mind As You Read And Study!

Assignment:

A. Text: Rev. 3:16

B. What Did Jesus Mean By "Lukewarm?"

C. What Did Jesus Mean By "I Would Thou Wert Cold Or Hot."

D. What Is The Problem?

E. What Tools Can You Use To Solve The Problem?

F. Using Your Tools, What Did Jesus Really Mean By "Lukewarm," And By "I Would Thou Wert Cold Or Hot."

Lesson Twelve

Specific Meaning Of Words: *"You Are Lukewarm, And Neither Cold Nor Hot"*

I. **Text:**
   A. Revelation 3:15-16

   B. "I Know Thy Works, That Thou Art Neither Cold Nor Hot: I Would Thou Wert Cold Or Hot. So Then Because Thou Art Lukewarm, And Neither Cold Nor Hot, I Will Spue Thee Out Of My Mouth." KJV

II. **The Problem:**
   A. One Might Ask, "What IS The Problem?" This Is Easy; Everyone Understands This Text.

   B. Question: What Does Jesus Mean When He Calls The Laodiceans "**LUKEWARM?**"

   C. Question: What Does Jesus Mean When He States His Wish That The Laodiceans Were Either "**COLD**" Or "**HOT?**"
      1. The difficulty is not that Jesus would prefer someone "**hot**" over someone "**lukewarm**."

2. But, why would He prefer someone **"cold"** over someone **"lukewarm?"**

III. Possible Interpretations

A. "Hot," "Cold," and "Lukewarm" Are Metaphors For The Spiritual Temperament Of Christians. Therefore, Jesus Is Stating That He Would Rather A Person Be "Cold" Spiritually Than "Lukewarm." He Is Calling Upon The Laodiceans To Make A Decision About Their True Intentions.

1. "Hot" — an active, "on fire" Christian.

2. "Cold" — a lazy, inactive Christian.

3. "Lukewarm" — an "indifferent" Christian.

B. "Hot," "Cold," and "Lukewarm" Are Used As Metaphors Referring To Circumstances Familiar To The Laodiceans.

IV. Tools To Use In Solving This Problem.

A. **Different Translations**.

B. Careful Examination Of The **Word Usage**.

C. Understanding The **Use Of Metaphors**.

D. Understanding The **Culture/Environment Of The Immediate Audience**.

E. **Context Of The Broader Passage** — What Else Is Happening During This Passage?

F. **Context Of The Immediate Passage** — Who Is Specifically Being Addressed?

V. **Using Your Tools To Evaluate And To Solve The Problem.**
    A. **Study Of Different Translations**.
        1. "I know thy works, that thou art neither cold nor hot: I would thou wert cold or hot. So because thou art lukewarm, and neither hot nor cold, I will spew thee out of my mouth." ASV

        2. "I know your works, that you are neither cold nor hot. I could wish you were cold or hot. So then, because you are lukewarm, and neither cold nor hot, I will vomit you out of My mouth." NKJV

        3. "I know your deeds, that you are neither cold nor hot. I wish you were either one or the other! So, because you are lukewarm—neither hot nor cold—I am about to spit you out of my mouth." NIV

        4. The study of different translations does not

really give much assistance; the only real help is the phrase "I could wish" or "I wish" instead of "I would."

B. **Careful Examination Of The Word Usage**.
1. In both verses, 15 and 16, the form in which the words "cold" and "hot" are presented indicates that they are to be seen as viable (acceptable) alternatives.

2. "Both "cold" and "hot" are used in a POSITIVE sense; they are NOT mentioned in a negative light!
    a. "**I would thou wert cold or hot**." KJV. "I could wish you were cold or hot." NKJV 15
    b. "So then because thou art lukewarm, and **neither cold nor hot**, I will spue thee out of my mouth." KJV 16
        1. Observe, He would not spew them out if they were either hot or cold!
        2. He is about to spew them out because they are lukewarm.
    c. If these words are metaphors for spiritual temperament, is it true that "cold" and "hot" are viewed as viable equivalent states by Jesus?
        1. The answer would be "Obviously not."
        2. Everything we know about the appropriate attitude toward God tells us that He would prefer that we were hot.

3. Interpreting "cold" and "hot" as direct metaphors for describing spiritual temperament will cause a contradiction with other Scriptures.

C. **Use of Metaphors.**
   1. Bible students MUST NOT ASSUME that the metaphors WE USE and take for granted TODAY are also used by people in other cultures today or that they were used by people in other cultures centuries ago.

   2. The words "hot" (**"ζεστός" "dzestos"**) and "cold" (**"ψυχρός" "psuchros"**) in this passage are rarely found to describe people in any writings (including the Bible) at this time.
      a. Usage of "ζεστός"
         1. Searing by a **hot iron.** I Tim. 4:2 "Speaking lies in hypocrisy; having their conscience seared with a **hot iron;**"
         2. "Hot" as "boiling hot" in our texts; Rev. 3:15,16
         3. Almost all of the passages of the O.T. that have the English word "hot" use the Greek word **"θερμός"** ("thermos" warm) in the LXX.
      b. Usage of "ψυχρός"
         1. **Cold weather.**
            a. Jn. 18:18 "And the servants and officers stood there, who had made a fire of coals; for **it was cold**: and they warmed themselves: and Peter stood with them, and warmed himself."

    b.   Ac. 28:2 "And the barbarous people showed us no little kindness: for **they kindled a fire**, and received us every one, because of the present rain, and **because of the cold**."

    c.   II Cor. 11:27 "In weariness and painfulness, in watchings often, in hunger and thirst, in fastings often, **in cold** and nakedness."

    d.   This word is also used in the LXX with this same usage:

        1.   Gen. 8:22 "While the earth remaineth, seedtime and harvest, and **cold** and heat, and summer and winter, and day and night shall not cease."

        2.   Job 24:7 "They cause the naked to lodge without clothing, that *they have* no covering **in the cold**."

        3.   Job 37:9 "Out of the south cometh the whirlwind: and **cold out of the north**."

        4.   Ps. 147:17 "He casteth forth his ice like morsels: who can stand before his **cold**?"

2. **Inactive faith**.

    a.   Mt. 24:12 "And because iniquity shall abound, the love of many shall wax **cold**."

    b.   Thayer alludes to this usage in his lexicon. Thayer, Joseph Henry. *Thayer's Greek-English*

Lexicon of the New Testament, Grand Rapids, MI: Zondervan, 1974, p. 678.

3. **Cool, refreshing water.**
   a. Mt. 10:42 "And whosoever shall give to drink unto one of these little ones a **cup of cold** *water* only in the name of a disciple, verily I say unto you, he shall in no wise lose his reward."
   b. This usage is seen in the O.T.:
      1. Pr. 25:13 "As the **cold** of snow in the time of harvest, *so is* a faithful messenger to them that send him: for he **refresheth** the soul of his masters."
      2. Pr. 25:25 "*As* **cold waters to a thirsty soul**, so *is* good news from a far country."
   c. **"Lukewarm"**
      1. This is the Greek word "χλιαρὸς" (chliaros).
      2. It is only used in Scripture in Rev. 3:16.
      3. According to some scholars, this would be the only case in ancient Greek literature where the word "lukewarm" would be applied directly to people.

3. For the most part, we see these words used are as adjectives describing weather or water.
   a. If these words are to be used as references to water, what is the metaphorical

connection to the church in Laodicea?"

    b. In order to understand the metaphor, we should seek to find some connection between Laodicea and water. How would the Laodiceans have understood "cold," "hot," and "lukewarm?"

D. **Understanding The Culture/Environment Of The Immediate Audience.**

    1. It is important for Bible students to remember that while the Bible is written so that its words apply to all mankind, much of it was written in an immediate context to specific people in specific places and times dealing with specific issues. In order for us to fully understand the full implications of a passage, we must become familiar with the culture of that initial audience.

    2. Often times, terms and phrases are used that have specific meaning to people in a certain location.

        a. An example:

            1. A common bumper sticker in Evansville — "Of course I'm late. I took the Lloyd!"

            2. You not only have to be familiar with Evansville, Indiana to understand this phrase, you have to have some familiarity with what life is like in Evansville to fully appreciate it.

            3. People who are not aware of the existence of the "Lloyd Expressway" and of all the stoplights on it would

not understand that the word "expressway" becomes almost a joke. An "expressway" should promote the flow of traffic, not restrict it.

b. Another example:
1. "The Bridge."
2. Mark Shifflet and I used to live in Michigan; he lived in the Upper Peninsula; I lived in the Lower Peninsula.
3. There is a huge bridge that connects the "U.P." and the "Lower Peninsula."
4. When people in the "U.P." speak of "The Bridge" they are speaking of the Mackinaw Bridge.
5. The phrase "The Bridge" would only cause confusion to people in most of the rest of the world.

3. The same thing can be said for some passages we read in the Bible.
a. How could "water" be understood metaphorically by the Laodiceans?
b. Laodicea was built with no natural water supply.
c. Two nearby communities had two different types of water supplies.
1. **Hieropolis** was known for its hot springs.
a. These waters were noted for their healing properties.
b. The waters were **extremely hot**.
2. **Colossae** was known for its **cold water** supply.

3. A primitive aqueduct was built between Hieropolis and Laodicea out of stone pipes. By the time the water reached Laodicea, it was usually in a lukewarm condition. The water would have to be left in jars overnight to cool it adequately.
4. Imagine having to live with a lukewarm water supply! The term lukewarm would certainly be relevant to the Laodiceans.

E. **Context of the Broader Passage.**
   1. This passage is the last of a series of letters to seven churches in Asia Minor.

   2. These letters were messages to those seven specific congregations; however, the scope is much greater than those seven congregations. The number "seven" in Jewish Apocalyptic literature stands for "perfection." Every congregation of the Lord's Church can be described in these seven letters.

   3. In several of these letters we see not only specific references to events in those churches but also the use of metaphors that would be understood clearly by people living in those communities.
      a. Rev. 2: 9 "**Synagogue of Satan.**"
         1. This letter was written to the church in Smyrna.
         2. This same phrase is used in the letter to Philadelphia. 3:9

3. Both communities were experiencing severe persecution that originated from the Jews in the local synagogues.

4. These Jews in the synagogues were "disciples of Satan" who opposed Christ and Christians by teaching Judaism and advocated obedience to the Law of Moses that had been nailed to the Cross by Christ.

b. Rev. 2:13 **"Satan's Seat [Throne]."**

1. This letter was written to the church in Pergamum.

2. Pergamum was not only a capital city serving the Roman government, it was also a pagan religious center promoting idolatrous paganism of Roman, Greek, and Asiatic backgrounds.

c. Rev. 2:14 **"the doctrine of Balaam."**

1. In Pergamum, some are accused of being those who "hold the doctrine of Balaam."

2. Balaam is the prophet that Balak, king of the Moabites, asked to curse Israel. Nu. 22-24; 31:16

3. God refused to allow Balaam to prophesy against Israel.

4. However, Balaam told Balak to use the Moabitish women to lead Israel's men into fornication.

5. In essence, Balaam told Balak that Israel could be destroyed by enticing them to compromise with Moab.

6. Some Christians in Pergamum were condoning idol worship and sensual immorality and encouraging the Christians to participate in these ungodly practices. Like Balaam, they were encouraging Christians to compromise Christian values.

d. Rev. 2:17 "And I will give him a **white stone**."

1. This message was also written to the church in Pergamum.

2. Possible suggestions of the "white stone" metaphor.

a. The winner of a race being given a stone to symbolize his victory over his opponents.

b. A stone given to a warrior who returns from defeating the enemies.

c. A stone of "acquittal" or "forgiveness" given to one acquitted in a trial. If so, the name might be "forgiven" or "justified."

3. Faithful Christians will have "victory in Jesus."

e. Rev. 2:20 "**Jezebel**"

1. This was written to the church at Thyatira.

2. "Trade guilds" almost ruled the city.

a. Each guild had its own idol.

b. They expected their employees to eat together.

c. Food offered to their idol gods was a part of their ritual.

d. Also lascivious action and fornication were a part of these rituals.

e. Failure to participate in these rituals or refusal to do so meant either ostracism or termination from employment.

3. This "Jezebel" was urging fellow Christians to participate in these wicked rituals.

f. Rev. 3:2,3 **"Be watchful..."**

1. This warning was written to the church in Sardis.

2. Sardis was built on a natural citadel, a cliff-like mountaintop on Mt. Tmolus.

3. It is known as a city that prided itself in its natural defenses; their arrogance caused them to be very lax in protecting the city.

4. Twice they were conquered because of a lack of attention.

a. 549 B.C. by Cyrus of Persia

b. 218 B.C. by Antiochus the Great of Greece

g. Rev. 3:12 "A **pillar** in the temple of my God."

1. This was written to the Christian in Philadelphia.

2. There were so many temples in this community that it had the title "Little Athens."

3. A prominent man might be honored with a pillar in the temple of his god.

4. Christ promises to make faithful Christians a "pillar" in the Temple of His God; likely this would mean a permanent place in Heaven.

F. **Immediate Context** (Letter to Laodiceans).
1. What does Jesus say about the Laodiceans?
   a. "Because thou sayest, I am **rich**, and increased with goods, and **have need of nothing**; and knowest not that thou art wretched, and miserable, and poor, and blind, and naked:" 3:17
      1. Laodicea, was known for its material wealth.
      2. It was a great banking center with strong ties to the Roman Empire.
      3. It was also a retirement center for wealthy retirees.
   b. Major industries were banking, eye salve called Phrygian powder, and clothing made from glossy-black wool.
      1. Their industries are alluded to in the text.
      2. "I counsel thee to buy of me **gold** tried in the fire, that thou mayest be rich; and **white raiment**, that thou mayest be clothed, and that the shame of thy nakedness do not appear; and anoint thine eyes with **eyesalve**, that thou mayest see." 3:18
   c. The Laodiceans took great pride in their self-reliance.
      1. When Laodicea, along with many other cities in the area, was severely

damaged by an earthquake, it did not seek any assistance from Rome to rebuild.

2. They could take care of every situation themselves.

3. Jesus quickly dispels this pride by pointing out the Laodicean's true condition. "Because thou sayest, I am rich, and increased with goods, and have need of nothing; and knowest not that thou art **wretched**, and **miserable**, and **poor**, and **blind**, and **naked**:" 3:17

4. Jesus' remedy for the "lukewarm" Laodiceans:

    a. 3:18 "I counsel thee to buy of me gold tried in the fire, that thou mayest be rich; and white raiment, that thou mayest be clothed, and *that* the shame of thy nakedness do not appear; and anoint thine eyes with eyesalve, that thou mayest see."

    b. His counsel:

        1. To the **poor**: "buy of me gold tried in the fire, that thou mayest be rich!"

        2. To the **naked**: "and white raiment, that thou mayest be clothed, and *that* the shame of thy nakedness do not appear."

        3. To the **blind**: "anoint thine eyes with eyesalve, that thou mayest see."

2. How does the metaphor reinforce Jesus' point?

   a. If we take the hot, cold and lukewarm to be referring to water, then the interpretation must coincide with the point Jesus is trying to make.

   b. The references must also be something that would immediately make sense to (have immediate meaning to) the Laodiceans.

   c. What do these various types of water provide?

Type of Water	Frame of Reference	Metaphorical Use
Hot water	Hieropolis (Hot Springs)	Spiritual Healing
Cold water	Colossae (Cold Water)	Spiritual Refreshment
Lukewarm water	Laodicea (Tepid Water)	Worthless, Disgusting

   d. Present-day examples to assist understanding:

   1. **"Hot water"** is refreshing and good to drink.
      a. Hot coffee
      b. Hot cocoa
      c. Hot tea

   2. **"Cold drinks"** can be extremely refreshing.
      a. Cold soft drinks
      b. Iced tea
      c. Icees

3. **"Lukewarm drinks"** are worthless and disgusting.
   a. "Tepid coffee" "Would you warm up my coffee?"
   b. "Lukewarm cocoa" It is not a drink one enjoys drinking.

e. In using these words in this sense, Jesus is saying to the Laodiceans that you may think very highly of yourselves but from my perspective, you are worthless, disgusting, nauseating, and sickening! A very powerful message to the church at Laodicea.

VI. Personal Application.

A. Question: Which Of The Seven Churches Of Asia Describes YOUR Congregation?

B. Do You Bring "Refreshing" And "Pleasure" To Christ, Or Do You "Disgust" Him?

C. Are You "Useful" To Him As You Exist As A Congregation, Or Are You Just "Keeping House" And Are "Worthless" To Him?

Suggested Study Material:

Mounce, Robert H. *The Book of Revelation*, Grand Rapids, MI: William B. Eerdmans Publishing Co, 1977, pp. 125,126.

Rudwick, M.J.S., and E.M.B. Green. "The Laodicean Lukewarmness," in *The Expository Times 69*, 1957-1958, pp. 176-178.

Assignment:

A. Text: Ac. 21:17-27

B. What Is The Problem In This Text?

C. What Are Possible Solutions To That Problem?

D. What Tools Can You Use To Solve This Problem?

E. Evaluate The Possible Solutions For The Answer That Seems Most Consistent With The Rest Of Scripture.

Culture And Seeming Contradiction

I. **The Text: Ac. 21:17-27**

II. **The Problem:**
- A. How Could James Advise Paul To Purify Himself And To Pay For The Four Men To Purify Themselves?

- B. How Could Paul Do This? It Seems To Be Against Everything That He Taught!

III. **Possible Answers To This Difficult Text:**
- A. Paul Was Acting Without Complete Revelation of God's Will.

- B. Paul Did Not Understand What He Had Taught Or Had Written By Inspiration.

- C. Paul Was Acting Hypocritically.

- D. Paul Just Did Not Follow The Advice Of James And The Elders.

E. Paul Compromised Principle For The Sake Of Unity.

F. Paul Was So Concerned For The Jews' Salvation That He Was Willing To Do ANYTHING To Win Them To Christ.

G. This Was The Advice Of James, Not The Elders!

H. Paul Made A Mistake In Judgment.

I. These 4 Men Had Just Recently Become Christians.

J. This Was An Interim Period Between The Law And The Gospel.

K. Paul Was Observing This As A National Custom Or Ritual, Not As A Way To Seek Grace Or Salvation.

IV. **Tools To Solve This Difficult Text:**
   A. The **Immediate Context**.

   B. The **Context Of Acts**.

C. **Study Of Paul's Epistles**.

D. **Evaluation Of Paul's Ethics**.

E. **Logical Evaluation Of Possible Answers In Light Of Biblical Knowledge**.

V. **Using Our Tools To Evaluate And To Solve The Problem**.
    A. **The Immediate Context**: Events Surrounding This Difficult Passage.
        1. Paul had returned to Jerusalem at the end of the Third Missionary Journey. 21:17

        2. He met with James and all the elders. 21:18

        3. He related the results of the Gospel among the Gentiles. 21:19

        4. They rejoiced at the response of the Gentiles. 21:20

        5. Then they related a problem to Paul. 21:20-21
            a. Many Jews have become Christians; however, they are still fervently attempting to hold on to the Law of Moses.
            b. These Jews have heard of Paul's teaching in which he encouraged the Gentiles to abandon all the requirements of the Law

of Moses, including circumcision and Jewish customs.

6. Their advice: 21:22-25
   a. These Jewish brethren will hear that you are in town.
   b. There are four men who have a vow on them. Take these four men, purify yourself, and pay the expenses for their purification so their heads can be shaven.

7. Their rationale: when these Jewish Christians see you do this, they will see that you are one who keeps the Law.

8. The next day, Paul took the four men and was purified along with them, suggesting that the vow was now to end. 21:26
   a. Paul himself had made a vow.
      1. Ac. 18:18 "having shorn *his* head in Cenchrea: for he had a vow."
      2. Some commentators try to apply this passage to Aquila, not Paul.
      3. The Vulgate holds this view; Adam Clark does too.
      4. However, in Ac. 18:18-25 there are 10 aorist participles. Each is a singular participle; all refer to Paul!
   b. Many assume that this was a Nazarite vow. Nu. 6:1-21.
      1. Some Nazarite vows lasted a week, some a month, some a set period designated by the vower, and some were for life.

2.   When the vow was finished, the one who made it would shave his head.

3.   If he were in a foreign land, the one who had made the vow would keep his hair and bring it to the Temple so that sacrifices could be made for him when he returned to Jerusalem. This must be what had happened to Paul.

4.   Paul later tells of this event and states that he WAS purified. Ac. 24:18 "Whereupon certain Jews from Asia found me purified in the temple, neither with multitude, nor with tumult."

5.   There is no evidence that Paul returned to Jerusalem from the time of Ac. 18, near the end of the Second Missionary Journey, about A.D. 54. The events of our present text, Acts 21, occurred about 4 or 5 years later, in A.D. 58. So, did he wait 4 or 5 years to be purified or to make a sacrifice that signified the end of the vow?

c.   Question: Could a Christian observe a Nazarite vow?

1.   What about the Nazarite requirement that "He shall separate *himself* from wine and strong drink, and shall drink no vinegar of wine, or vinegar of strong drink, neither shall he drink any liquor of grapes, nor eat moist grapes, or dried." Nu. 6:3

2.   How could a Christian observe the

Lord's Supper while keeping such a vow?

d. This seems to refer to a practice where the one who had made a vow went to the priest and made it known that he was about to end his vow.

1. Some suggest that he was to come to the Temple each day during that seven-day period.

2. Others suggest that one who made the vow would come to the Temple and inform the priest of his intention to end the vow. Then at the end of the seven days, he would shave his head and sacrifices would be made as required by the Nazarite law.

b. They seem to be following the requirements of the Law of Moses.

c. At the end of 7 days, the sacrifice was to be made ending the vow. Nu. 6:9

9. As the 7 days were about to end, the Jews of Asia saw Paul and stirred up the people of Jerusalem against him. 21:27-30

a. Their accusations:

1. Paul opposes EVERYTHING about Judaism — the Jewish people, the Law, and the Temple!

2. He brought Greeks into the Temple, thus desecrating or profaning it!

a. They had seen Trophimus with Paul in the city of Jerusalem.

b. Then they jumped to the conclusion that Paul had taken Trophimus into the Temple.

  c. This was a charge punishable by death. Josephus. *Antiquities of the Jews*, Book xv, chapter xi, verse 5; Wars of the Jews, book v, chapter v, verse 2; *Wars of the Jews*, book vi, chapter ii, verse 4.

 b. These accusations were merely prejudicial accusations!

10. Paul's conversation with the chief captain. 21:31-40

 a. As this angry mob was about to kill Paul, a report came to the chief captain of the Roman Garrison stationed in Jerusalem.

  1. This was Claudius Lysias. 23:26

  2. He ordered Paul to be bound with two chains; then Claudius Lysias demanded what Paul had done!

 b. Because there was so much confusion being caused by the mob and many conflicting accusations, the chief captain could not understand the truth; therefore he took Paul into the fort called Antonia.

 c. Soldiers literally carried Paul as they tried to save him from the angry mob.

 d. As they got Paul to the top of the steps, he said to the chief captain, "May I say something to you?"

  1. The chief captain was amazed that Paul spoke Greek.

  2. He had assumed that Paul was an Egyptian who had led a band of 4,000 murdering assassins into the wilderness. That assassin had killed many in Jerusalem including the High Priest.

3. Paul explained to him that he was a Jew of Tarsus of Cilicia.
4. He begged the chief captain to allow him to speak to the mob.
5. Paul then addressed the crowd in Hebrew. Chapter 22

B. **The Context Of Acts**.
1. The First Missionary Journey was from A.D. 45-47. Acts 13:4-14:28

2. The Second Missionary Journey was from A.D. 50-54. Acts 15:40-18:22

3. The Third Missionary Journey was from A.D. 54-58. Acts 18:23-21:17
   a. Paul wrote **I Corinthians** during the two years he was at Ephesus. Ac. 19:10
   b. He wrote **II Corinthians** while in Macedonia. Ac. 20:1
   c. While in Greece for 3 months, Paul wrote **Galatians** and **Romans**. Ac. 20:3
   d. During the Second Missionary Journey, Paul had Timothy circumcised.
      1. Ac. 16:1-3 "Then came he to Derbe and Lystra: and, behold, a certain disciple was there, named Timotheus, the son of a certain woman, which was a Jewess, and believed; but his father *was* a Greek: ²Which was well reported of by the brethren that were at Lystra and Iconium. ³Him would Paul have to go forth with him; and took and

circumcised him because of the Jews
which were in those quarters: for
they knew all that his father was a
Greek."
2. Timothy's mother was a Jew; his
father was a Greek.
3. Likely this was for the purpose of
having greater influence among the
Jews.
e. However, during the Third Missionary
Journey, Paul wrote about Jews
demanding that Titus be circumcised; he
absolutely and resolutely refused!
1. Gal. 2:3-5 "But neither Titus, who
was with me, being a Greek, was
compelled to be circumcised: ⁴And
that because of false brethren
unawares brought in, who came in
privily to spy out our liberty which
we have in Christ Jesus, that they
might bring us into bondage: ⁵To
whom we gave place by subjection,
no, not for an hour; that the truth of
the gospel might continue with you."
2. When Jews demanded that Titus
HAD TO BE circumcised, Paul
bowed his back and did not budge!
f. Keep in mind that Paul had already
written:
1. II Cor. 3:6-11
2. Gal. 1:1–5:6
3. Rom. 1-8
4. How could he have written these
things and then contradicted them?

C. **Study Of Paul's Epistles**.
1. He declared that the Law of Moses was dead!
   a. Rom. 7:1-7
   b. Eph. 2:15
   c. Col. 2:14

2. He proclaimed the superiority of the New Covenant of Christ over the Law of Moses. That is the message of the book of Hebrews.

3. He showed the sinfulness of attempting to follow both the teaching of the Law of Moses and the Gospel of Christ simultaneously.
   a. Rom. 7:3,4
   b. Gal. 5:1-6

D. **Evaluation Of Paul's Ethics**.
1. Paul was NOT a compromiser! He would suffer and die for his beliefs.
   a. He endured hatred, persecution, and imprisonment, yet he would not compromise his convictions!
      1. At Antioch of Pisidia the Jews contradicted Paul and blasphemed him. Ac. 13:45
      2. At Lystra, he was stoned and left for dead. Ac. 14:19
      3. At Philippi, he was scourged and imprisoned. Ac. 16:23,24
      4. At Ephesus a mob rioted against Paul's condemnation of idolatry. Ac. 19:21-41
      5. When he arrived in Jerusalem in Ac. 21, the Jews were determined to kill him.

    b.   Gal. 2:3-5 He was adamant that Judaizers would not circumcise Titus.

    c.   He had NO shame for the Gospel. Rom. 1:16; II Tim. 1:12

2.   He would call upon close friends to repent. Peter. Gal. 2:11-21 (especially 11).

E.   **Logical Evaluation Of Possible Answers** In Light Of Biblical Knowledge.

   1.   **Paul was acting without complete revelation of God's Will!**

      a.   Those who hold this view suggest that Paul had not yet written Ephesians and Hebrews.

      b.   Yet, he had the mind of God! I Cor. 2:16 "But we have the mind of Christ."

      c.   He knew enough to straighten out the Apostles in Jerusalem! Ac. 15

   2.   **Paul did not understand what he had taught or written by inspiration.**

      a.   This makes Paul ignorant of the inspired message!

      b.   He surely seems to have understood previously! Eph. 3:3-5

   3.   **Paul was acting hypocritically!**

      a.   There is NO evidence that this is true!

      b.   Remember, Paul said two chapters later, "I have lived in all good conscience before God **until this day.**" Ac. 23:1 So, HAD HE OR NOT??

c. If he had lived in all good conscience until that day, it means he had lived in good conscience in chapter 21!

4. **Paul just did not follow the advice of James and the Elders.**
   a. This seems to contradict the events that occur in the text.
   b. Paul DID do as James suggested, verse 26; He did not get to finish the seven day purification because of the mob, verse 27.
   c. An interesting question is, "What did they mean by, 'Show that you **keep** the law.'"
      1. This is not the word for obey it.
      2. The Greek word "φυλάσσων" (fulassoon) means "to guard" or "to place a watch on."
         a. It may be used metaphorically for keeping a law.
         b. But that is a metaphorical sense.
      3. The Greek noun for "obedience" is "ὑπακοή" (hupakoa); the Greek verb for "obey" is "ὑπακούω" (hupakouoo).

5. **Paul compromised principle for the sake of unity!**
   a. Paul was NOT a compromiser!
   b. Had he compromised, he would have surrendered the very Will of God!

6. **Paul was so concerned for the Jews' salvation that he was willing to do ANYTHING to win them to Christ.**

  a. It is true that Paul had great concern for the people of his own nation.

  b. His concern was clearly expressed:

    1. Rom. 9:2,3 "I have great heaviness and continual sorrow in my heart. ³For I could wish that myself were accursed from Christ for my brethren, my kinsmen according to the flesh:"

    2. Rom. 10:1 "Brethren, my heart's desire and prayer to God for Israel is, that they might be saved."

  c. However, Paul would not do ANYTHING!

7. **This was the advice of James, not the elders!**

  a. This is compared with Gal. 2:11ff.

    1. 2:11-14 "But when Peter was come to Antioch, I withstood him to the face, because he was to be blamed. ¹²For before that **certain came from James**, he did eat with the Gentiles: but when they were come, he withdrew and separated himself, fearing them which were of the circumcision. ¹³And the other Jews dissembled likewise with him; insomuch that Barnabas also was carried away with their dissimulation. ¹⁴But when I saw that they walked not uprightly according to the truth of the gospel, I said unto Peter before *them* all, If thou, being a Jew, livest after the manner of Gentiles, and not as do the Jews, why

compellest thou the Gentiles to live as do the Jews?"

2. Events:

   a. Peter was fellowshipping Gentile brethren in Antioch; he was not expecting them to practice O.T. customs at all.

   b. When some Jewish brethren came down **from James** at Jerusalem, Peter stopped eating with the Gentiles because of his fear of the Jews.

   c. He influenced many others; even Barnabas.

   d. Paul condemned Peter for not walking according to the Truth of the Gospel!

   e. Perhaps James had not fully grasped the significance of the Gospel and the fact that the Old Law was now annulled.

   f. If true, he seemed to be encouraging Paul to show that he, a Christian, still adhered to the Law of Moses.

   g. Of course, Paul had strongly taught that Christians do not and cannot adhere to the Law!

b. James was suggesting that if Paul would follow their advice, the Jews would be willing to listen to him.

c. Verses 20,23 do not suggest that it was just the advice of James!

   1. "And when **they heard** *it*, **they glorified** the Lord, and **said** unto

him, Thou seest, brother, how many thousands of Jews there are which believe; and they are all zealous of the law:" 20
2. "Do therefore this that **we say** to thee: **We have** four men which have a vow on them;" 23
3. All these verbs are plural, not singular!

8. **Paul made a mistake in judgment.**
   a. This view suggests that he erred as Peter did in Gal. 2.
   b. Further, this view must espouse that he did wrong, even though he did not feel guilty about doing it.
      1. He affirmed later that he had lived in all good conscience unto THAT day!
      2. Ac. 23:1 "And Paul, earnestly beholding the council, said, Men *and* brethren, I have lived in all good conscience before God until this day."
      3. Ac. 24:16 "And herein do I exercise myself, to have always a conscience void of offence toward God, and *toward* men."
   c. Thus, the suggestion would be that he was sinning ignorantly as he did when he was persecuting the Church and Christians. I Tim. 1:13 "Who was before a blasphemer, and a persecutor, and injurious: but I obtained mercy, because I did *it* ignorantly in unbelief."

9. **These 4 men had just recently become Christians.**
   a. This view says they had made the vow before becoming Christians.
   b. That is not stated.
   c. Further, what about Paul participating? He was not a recent convert!

10. **This was an interim period between the Law and the Gospel.**
    a. This was a time when people were going from the Law of Moses unto the Gospel of Christ.
    b. So, God was tolerant as things were going from one system to another.
    c. It is true that the Old Law had been abolished. Eph. 2:15; Col. 2:14.
    d. However, the Temple still stood and Jewish worship continued.
       1. Christ's prophecy in Mt. 24 declared that the Temple and the surrounding buildings would be destroyed.
       2. Paul asserted that the Temple and Its worship were about to "vanish away!"
          a. Heb. 8:13 "In that he saith, A new *covenant*, he hath made the first old. Now that which decayeth and waxeth old *is* ready to vanish away." KJV
          b. NIV "By calling this covenant "new," he has made the first one obsolete; and what is obsolete and aging will soon disappear."

3. II Cor. 3:7-11 says, "But if the ministration of death, written *and* engraven in stones, was glorious, so that the children of Israel could not stedfastly behold the face of Moses for the glory of his countenance; which *glory* was to be done away: [8]How shall not the ministration of the spirit be rather glorious? [9]For if the ministration of condemnation *be* glory, much more doth the ministration of righteousness exceed in glory. [10]For even that which was made glorious had no glory in this respect, by reason of the glory that excelleth. [11]For if **that which is done away** *was* glorious, much more that which remaineth *is* glorious." KJV

   a. ASV "that which passeth away"
   b. NIV "what was fading away"
   c. Greek "the thing being done away"
      1. Present, passive!
      2. It was continuing to be done away.
      3. This is the same word as "abolished" in Eph. 2:15

e. This view claims that it was not fully abolished or terminated until the destruction of Jerusalem.

11. **Paul was observing this as a national custom or ritual, not as a way to seek grace or salvation.**

a. He had previously shaved his head. Ac. 18:18

b. This was still considered part of the Jewish "Civil Law," however, it was not "God's Law" that was now in effect.

1. The Law of Moses had ended at the Cross.

2. Paul was well aware of this; he knew that this had nothing to do with obeying God!

c. Paul did not condemn Jews who chose to be circumcised, as long as they understood that it was of no value in God's sight because it was no longer binding.

d. Paul did it as a Jewish custom, NOT as obedience to the Law.

1. I Cor. 9:20 "And unto the Jews I became as a Jew, that I might gain the Jews; to them that are under the law, as under the law, that I might gain them that are under the law;"

2. I Cor. 9:21-23 "To them that are without law, as without law, (being not without law to God, but under the law to Christ,) that I might gain them that are without law. ²²To the weak became I as weak, that I might gain the weak: I am made all things to all *men*, that I might by all means save some. ²³And this I do for the gospel's sake, that I might be partaker thereof with *you*,"

3. Col. 2:20-22 "Wherefore if ye be dead with Christ from the rudiments

of the world, why, as though living in the world, are ye subject to ordinances, [21](Touch not; taste not; handle not; [22]Which all are to perish with the using;) after the commandments and doctrines of men? [23]Which things have indeed a show of wisdom in will worship, and humility, and neglecting of the body; not in any honour to the satisfying of the flesh."

Conclusion:
- A. Sometimes We May Really Struggle To Comprehend Certain Actions In The Lives Of Biblical People.

- B. Before Accusing One Of Sin, We Need To Carefully Consider As Many Alternatives As Possible.

- C. This Lesson Surely Reminds Us Of The Struggles That Can Occur In Our Lives Between God's Truth And Culture. May We Always Strive To Uphold God's Truth Above All Else!

Final Comments

I commend you for your working through these lessons. It is my prayer that you have become a much better student of God's Word. I trust that you have found the thrill of studying and learning God's Truths. Several older Christians have told me, "This is the best Bible Class I have ever attended. One fine Christian woman told me, "I really learned a lot. I knew some of the final conclusions, but not the process of figuring it out. I now have confidence to try to figure out things I don't understand when I study instead of skipping over it." Hopefully you have learned about more tools to assist you and have gained tremendous confidence in your ability to study.

Mark Shifflet and I have already taught a second series of "Difficult Passages" to our students here at Washington Avenue. I plan to publish another book entitled "*How To Study Difficult Passages Of The Bible #2*". More very challenging lessons will be presented in it.

One of my favorite questions to my students is this, "Are you having any fun yet?" I hope you can answer a resounding, "YES!" May you always cherish the study of the precious, inspired Word of God and be more and more eager to learn Its Divine Truths!